WITH 266 ILLUSTRATIONS IN FULL COLOR

GAMEBIRDS

A GUIDE TO NORTH
AND THE

by

ALEXANDER SPRUNT IV
Research Director, National Audubon Society

and

HERBERT S. ZIM, Ph.D., Sc.D.

Illustrated by

JAMES GORDON IRVING

 GOLDEN PRESS • NEW YORK
Western Publishing Company, Inc.
Racine, Wisconsin

FOREWORD

Since the earliest days, men have hunted. Today about 12 million hunters buy licenses in the United States, and most hunt gamebirds. These larger birds are equally interesting to those who hunt with a camera and to those who just enjoy looking at birds.

Hunting regulations impose on the hunter the responsibility of identifying a gamebird before he shoots. Recognition of rare and protected species is the first step in keeping them alive. For these reasons and many others we have brought into the Golden Guide Series a book of basic data on American gamebirds. In so doing we have had invaluable assistance from Robert P. Allen and Alexander Sprunt, Jr., ornithologists of note. The experience of Grace Crowe Irving with western birds was valuable, as was the help of Donna Nelson Sprunt in the preparation of the manuscript. The artist joins us in thanking Charles E. O'Brien and Joseph O'Connell of the American Museum of Natural History.   A.S., IV; H.S.Z.

HOW TO USE THE RANGE MAPS IN THIS BOOK

Beginning with the Canada Goose on page 22, you will find range maps for most birds. The areas where the birds breed are shown in red; the areas where they winter are shown in blue. The areas in purple show where the summer and winter ranges overlap or where the birds are resident. When the ranges of two birds are shown on the same map, one bird's range is shown in solid colors, the other in blue and red lines.

CONTENTS

INTRODUCING GAMEBIRDS

A great number of birds have been considered game in years past. Everything from flamingos to hummingbirds have been taken for food, sport, or even for medicinal use. In North America many species now rigidly protected were shot regularly years ago. Robins, meadowlarks, bobolinks, and a host of other small birds were sought for the pot when our great-grandfathers took to the field. Nowadays, with hunting far more important as recreation than as a source of food, our ideas of gamebirds have changed. What we call gamebirds are still birds that are good eating, but they are also birds with the wildness, fast flight, and elusiveness that appeal to sportsmen. Despite reasonable hunting by men, a game species is able to maintain itself.

Modern sportsmen are well aware of their responsibility to conserve game species. Season and bag limits are a recognized essential. Fees for licenses and stamps, and taxes on arms and ammunition help provide funds for wildlife research and for development of refuges where game species can breed, or where they can rest and feed during migration. Several federal and state agencies and a number of non-profit organizations work steadily on the problems of protecting our gamebird population.

The value of gamebirds goes far beyond their appeal to sportsmen. They are important links in the biologic food chain that includes all living things—hunters and hunted. Many people who do not hunt find gamebirds a special delight. All watch their coming and going with the changing seasons and thrill to the sight of pheasants rising above corn shocks, and to the honking of geese high overhead.

CLASSIFICATION OF GAMEBIRDS. Gamebirds are not a natural group of birds. Those of North America fall into 12 different families. Since gamebirds are hunted, and hunting is regulated by law, the definition is a legal one —but one that has been changed continually since Connecticut first set up hunting seasons in 1677. Effective large-scale regulation of hunting, less than a century old, is based on international cooperation. A migratory bird treaty with Canada was ratified in 1918 and one with Mexico in 1936. These establish federal or national jurisdiction over migratory birds. Many gamebirds migrate and hence are under federal control. The federal government establishes basic regulations and states may make modification within these limits. The various states (the provinces in Canada) have direct responsibility for non-migratory gamebirds. This distinction, though legally clear, does not fit the natural picture perfectly. Some migratory birds may be found the year round in parts of their range. Some non-migratory species move locally with the seasons, or with changes in the food supply.

MIGRATORY GAMEBIRDS include all the waterfowl (ducks, geese and swans), the cranes, rails, shorebirds, doves and pigeons. These are the groups named in the treaties with Canada and Mexico. Responsibility for them is given the U.S. Department of the Interior through its Fish and Wildlife Service. The treaty provides that birds in all of these groups may be hunted, but, in actual practice, the list of available species is limited. Rare species and those which have been depleted by overshooting or for other reasons are removed from the list. If and when their population rises to a safe level, they are listed once more. Thus, the open season list of gamebirds varies from year to year with changing conditions. After a careful annual survey, the regulations for the coming year are distributed by the Fish and Wildlife Service. When the local situation warrants it, states may impose stricter regulations.

FLYWAYS AND MIGRATION ROUTES are clearly established for many migrating birds. Birds moving south in fall and north in spring do not move at random in these general directions. Many species, especially waterfowl, move along four major migratory paths or flyways. Research, based largely on bird banding (p. 9), discloses these patterns. The flyways are not rigid. Both to the north and south they overlap and are not well defined. But, across the United States, they are more pronounced. Certain populations of birds tend to migrate together and follow the same flyway year after year. This tendency of certain groups of birds within a species to stay together makes them more vulnerable to overshooting. Concentration of migrating gamebirds may be much greater in one flyway than in another. Factors involved are the success of the nesting season, available food, weather, and hunting pressure. Regulations on migratory gamebirds are is-

NORTH AMERICAN FLYWAYS

sued in terms of flyways and flyway boundaries have been adjusted to state lines for the convenience of law enforcement. Both state and federal law enforcement agents cooperate in enforcing game laws. Best known of these officers are state game wardens and U.S. Game Management Agents.

REGULATIONS protect the breeding stock of migratory gamebirds and insure a continued supply in years to come. In order to provide for both the present and the future, regulations must be adjusted to meet new conditions. Field biologists travel hundreds of thousands of miles all over North America to gather data. They start with a continent-wide census after the hunting season and continue into the next breeding season. They can then estimate how many birds have been killed, how many have returned north, and how many young have been raised. These facts are presented at an annual summer conference. Fish and Wildlife experts evaluate the situation and propose regulations for the coming year. Representatives of sportsmen's groups, conservation agencies, and other interested parties present their opinions, too. Thus, everyone interested enough in gamebirds to belong to one of the cooperating groups can play a part in establishing regulations. When all have been heard, the Fish and Wildlife Service experts face the difficult task of resolving differences of opinion and of making the regulations. Regulations are made on a North American basis. Sometimes local concentrations of a bird with a closed season give an erroneous impression of abundance.

Making an aerial census of waterfowl in the Arctic.

Biologists making brood counts.

RESEARCH on gamebird populations, distribution, habits, and diseases is carried out by federal and state agencies, universities, museums, and conservation organizations. A major instrument of research is bird banding. Banding consists of placing a small aluminum band on the leg of a bird. Each band has a serial number and requests that the finder return it to the U.S. Fish and Wildlife Service, Washington 25, D. C. The success of bird banding has been due to two kinds of cooperation. Most of the banding is done by highly qualified amateurs who have special permits to live-trap birds and band them. Many young birds are banded in the nest. As soon as the band is attached, a record of the number, identification, place and date are sent to Washington. The finder who turns in the band is equally important. He is asked to flatten it out and send it in with the place and date found, and the cause of the bird's death, if known. If the finder sends along his own name and address, he will be informed when and where the bird was banded. Many banded birds are also retrapped and released by banders along migration routes or when they return to their nesting grounds.

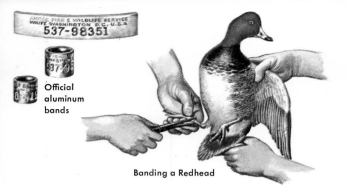

Official
aluminum
bands

Banding a Redhead

The simple device of banding millions of birds has yielded remarkable information. It gave the first reliable figures on longevity of birds in the wild. Banding data has established mortality ratios so that experts can now estimate the percentage of survival of any year's crop of gamebirds for each year that follows. Most important of all, banding has enabled scientists to trace migration routes and to discover how many birds fly thousands of miles back and forth from their breeding grounds to wintering areas. The flyway pattern (p. 7) emerged from a study of bird banding data over a period of years. Fifty years of bird banding have proved the importance of this research but many questions still remain unanswered.

Hunters and bird watchers may see other identifying marks on gamebirds. Sometimes there is a colored plastic band around a leg in addition to the aluminum one. Sometimes the wings, neck, or the entire bird is dyed a bright color such as yellow or red. These types of markings are used in several research projects. If such a marked bird is seen or killed, report it to the Fish and Wildlife Service or to your local game warden. Your cooperation is an essential part of wildlife research.

Dyed
Mourning
Dove

Canada Goose
dyed and collared

"Bowties"
on Bobwhite

REFUGE SYSTEMS are essential to the survival of migratory gamebirds. Growing from a single area set aside in 1903, the system now includes close to 300 National Wildlife Refuges. Over 200 of these are specifically for waterfowl, and fall into three general groups—nesting areas, resting grounds along the flyways, and wintering grounds where birds can find food and shelter. Refuges range in size from small, coastal islands of a few acres to huge tracts of almost 4,000 sq. miles. On these areas, which are often improved for wildlife use, birds find food, shelter, and frequently a helping hand from the manager and staff. State conservation agencies and private organizations, such as the National Audubon Society, also maintain refuges, many of which are for gamebirds. The National Parks are refuges also, since no hunting of any kind is permitted in them. Most national, state and organizational refuges are open to the public. Visitors are welcomed and such a trip is a rewarding experience. Make inquiries in advance. (List of Refuges on p. 157.)

Dyed Lesser Scaups

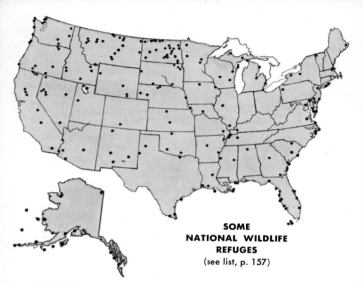

**SOME
NATIONAL WILDLIFE
REFUGES**
(see list, p. 157)

NON-MIGRATORY GAMEBIRDS—quail, grouse, pheasants, and turkeys—present a different set of problems. Control and protection are localized since the birds do not ordinarily move long distances across state or national boundaries. But, because of their more limited movements, non-migratory birds are more susceptible to overshooting, habitat destruction, and other factors. In most areas the numbers of non-migratory gamebirds had been greatly reduced. Only constant vigilance has produced the local, small increases. Though wild areas are decreasing in size, some compensation through habitat improvement (p. 154) is possible. Hunting regulations are set by the states and Canadian provinces, usually in consultation with sportsmen and conservation groups.

Though their sedentary nature makes the management of non-migratory gamebirds somewhat easier, the problem of habitat destruction has assumed major importance. Many waterfowl breed in the northern wilderness where there is less human competition for land use. The breeding grounds of the turkey have become farms, fields and towns in the northeastern states. With less and less land available for gamebirds, there is a shortage of food and shelter, and more disturbance of nests and young. State conservation agencies work with farmers and land owners, showing them how sub-marginal land and woodlots can be improved for wildlife production. Habitat improvement is also part of the program of major lumber and paper companies, and ranchers with large tracts of land. The U.S. Forest Service carries on its own wildlife program.

Attempts to supplement the supply of these desirable birds by releasing pen-raised individuals have now been replaced by research programs on longevity, movements, food and shelter requirements, and disease. These are already yielding a larger crop of wild birds. Upland gamebirds are all highly prized by sportsmen and their active cooperation helps insure a steady crop.

GAMEBIRDS AND YOU. Gamebirds are a national resource that belongs to all people—not just to hunters or bird watchers. Everyone who spends time out-of-doors can have his life made richer by the sight and sounds of these handsome creatures. There are still places where wild turkey gobblers can be seen strutting among the pines, and in the autumn a covey of quail may burst from a southern roadside thicket. Sportsmen have long known that game laws make good hunting possible. However, the broader problems of conservation and long-range land use are just as important. Your heritage of wildlife merits your personal attention to local, state and national conservation issues.

GAMEBIRD WEIGHTS AND RECORDS intrigue every hunter. There is no single way to determine the size of a gamebird. Weight is the most practical, but even this is inadequate. The age of a bird, its subspecies and sex influence weight. So do the season, weather, location, and even the time of day. Common ducks, geese, quail and pheasants have been weighed and studied so reliable figures of *average* weights are available. Average weights for most other gamebirds given in this book are based on limited data. Much more research is needed.

Record weights are much less satisfactory. There are no "official records" as there is no group which authenticates and records bird weights. If you shoot what you think is a record bird, try the following suggestions:

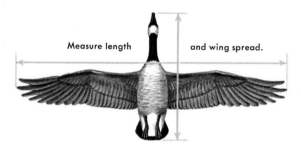

Measure length and wing spread.

KEEPING GAMEBIRD RECORDS
1. Weigh, measure and take all notes before dressing bird.
2. Get down pertinent data—identification, sex (if possible), where and when shot, circumstances, others in party, addresses.
3. Photograph the bird, wings outstretched, lying on a smooth surface.
4. Take measurements as in the diagram above; sketch and record.
5. Take your bird to the nearest game warden, conservation agent, or refuge manager. Ask him to check identification, measurements and weight.
6. Weigh the bird to the nearest half ounce on an inspected commercial scale. As a favor, a postmaster might weigh your bird on a post office scale and give you a signed statement of its weight.

EXTINCT AND THREATENED SPECIES

Dodo

Thousands of kinds of birds have become extinct during past ages as part of the natural process of evolution. But, during the last 500 years, the human population has increased explosively, and this aggressive species imposes a special threat to many others. Because the human population is still climbing rapidly, this problem will get worse. Yet, for our own good, scientists are paying more and more attention to ways of preserving important animals. Some birds, mammals, and fishes have been hunted and trapped in such numbers that their existence has become threatened. The Dodo, a 40-pound, flightless pigeon, is one famous bird that became extinct about 1680. Other gamebirds (pp. 16-17) have followed. Still others are limited in number and are threatened species. Some, not in families treated later, are shown on pp. 18-19. A few are repeated in their families for comparison. That concerted action can save threatened species has been demonstrated time and time again. Control of hunting and shooting is a first line of defense. Of far greater importance is the preservation and development of breeding and feeding grounds where threatened species can live normal lives.

Passenger Pigeons

15

EXTINCT BIRDS

Since the Dodo disappeared about 1680, nearly one hundred species and subspecies of birds have become extinct, and another 20 are probably extinct. Parrots, rails, Hawaiian honeycreepers, pigeons, ducks, and quails have suffered the most.

LABRADOR DUCKS became extinct in 1875. For the previous decade they were rare; earlier they were never common. They wintered along the Atlantic coast from Maine to New Jersey. Labrador Ducks were birds of bays, inlets and sand bars. They were wary and difficult to shoot. Occasionally hunters bagged enough to send to market, but the birds were poor eating and were not specially hunted. Why the Labrador Duck became extinct is still a question, but even minor factors can become serious when the species population is small.

ESKIMO CURLEW is sometimes confused with the Hudsonian Curlew, so reports that the bird still lives are sometimes received. Many experts believe it has been extinct for about 20 years. This bird bred in the tundra of northern

Canada and migrated out over the Atlantic to winter in the Argentine pampas. In fall it was hunted in Bermuda, and in spring thousands were killed in the prairie states. Perhaps Eskimo raids on the nesting grounds, perhaps hurricanes during migration have contributed to its extinction. At any rate, this curlew is extinct or near extinction.

PASSENGER PIGEONS were, in colonial times and later, so abundant in central U.S. that they were continually used for food. They lived in the East and South also, but not in as great numbers. The great colonial nesting grounds in the Midwest in beech, maple and oak forests contained millions, perhaps billions of birds. Indians used fire to kill nesting birds; later market hunters used dynamite. The cutting of forests and uncontrolled hunting doomed these birds. After 1850 the large colonial nestings were fewer; by the 1880's the birds were rare, and the last one died in a Cincinnati zoo in 1914. This was a valuable species which has left a gap in our gamebird population.

HEATH HEN was an eastern form of the Greater Prairie Chicken (p. 124). The Heath Hen was hunted as a table and market bird from colonial times in New England and south to New Jersey. The hunting, and the opening of farm land, so reduced the population that steps to protect Heath Hens were taken as early as 1791. By 1840 the bird was rare and by 1870 it was gone from the mainland. A small colony persisted on Martha's Vineyard—increasing under protection to about 2,000 in 1916. Then a fire destroyed most of the birds and the rest of the population rapidly declined. By 1931 a single bird remained. It soon lived out its protected life. The western form still occurs in reduced numbers in Kansas, Nebraska and other prairie states.

Trumpeter Swan

Ross' Goose

THREATENED SPECIES may still be saved though the problem is seldom simple. Often several interrelated conditions have reduced the bird populations; then, any single one may be decisive. After a certain critical point, the bird is doomed even though some survivors remain. This

WHITE PELICAN, though 5 ft. long with a 9 ft. wingspread, is sometimes mistaken for the Snow Goose by hunters. One look at its bill will eliminate this error. The White Pelican is much less common than the Brown. It breeds in western lakes from Calif. to Canada and, in fall, migrates to the Gulf Coast and Florida. All the birds on this page are completely protected and should never be shot.

ROSS' GOOSE (23 in.) is the smallest N.A. goose — no larger than a duck. It is found with Snow Geese but is distinctly smaller and has a smaller, red, warty bill. It breeds north of the Arctic Circle in Canada and winters in the valleys of central California. It was once common, and heavily hunted.

SWANS are among the largest waterfowl, and the Trumpeter Swan is our largest species. This bird has been saved from extinction, though it is still a threatened species. Its breeding grounds have extended and the chances for its survival are much better than a decade ago. This 5½ ft. long white bird has a black bill. It may be confused with the smaller Whistling Swan (4 ft.) which migrates through the same area of the northern Rockies. Both birds feed mainly on water plants and nest close to the water. In the East, the Mute Swan, with an orange bill, is an introduced bird which occasionally goes wild. All species of swans are rigidly protected by law. It is a good practice not to shoot any large all-white bird.

White Pelican

Whooping Crane

critical point varies with the kind of bird, its feeding habits, nesting habits, migrations, and other factors. Total planning for the best use of all land, and the maintenance of ample reserves of "useless" lands in their natural state are essential for preserving these species.

WHOOPING CRANE has become a symbol of a heroic effort to save an outstanding species. Its numbers are so low that a single disaster could wipe out the species, for the total Whooping Crane population has remained between 20 and 40 during the past 30 years. The birds nest in northern Canada and winter along the Gulf Coast in Texas. Coming, going, and at all times between, these large 5 ft. birds are watched carefully. Note the red face, black wing tips and all-white body. Young birds are brownish. Space is of paramount importance in the preservation of this species. Adequate isolated habitat must be provided at both ends of the migration route in northern Alberta and along the Texas coast near Corpus Christi.

BLACK-BELLIED TREE DUCKS range from Mexico into southern Texas and rarely into N. Mex. and Ariz. They perch in trees along ponds and lakes and feed in corn fields. Related to the Fulvous Tree Duck (p. 33), this pink-billed, black-bellied species with large white wing patches is rare in U.S., but is still common in Mexico and Central America.

Black-bellied
Tree Duck

WATERFOWL

Swans, geese, and ducks make up the waterfowl (family *Anatidae*). Of over 200 species, some 45 are native to North America. From earliest times these birds have been important, first, as a source of food, more recently, for sport. Their down and feathers have stuffed many a pillow and comforter. Goose quills were the ball-point pens of past centuries. Waterfowl give as much pleasure to the millions who watch them and study their habits as they do to the sportsmen who hunt them.

SWANS: Snow-white color; very large size; very long neck; bill flattened but high at the base; feed by "tipping up" in shallow water; in taking flight, they rise from water only after running along surface. Male and female similar in color. (p. 18)

GEESE: Sexes alike in color; neck shorter than swans but longer than ducks; bill high, not flattened; feed on land and in water by "tipping up"; in taking flight, rise after a short run. Characteristics intermediate between ducks and swans. (pp. 22-33)

Whistling Swan

Canada Goose

All waterfowl share certain features which affirm their relationship. Some of these are: (1) Bill usually flattened with small, tooth-like edges; (2) Four toes on each foot, three webbed and the fourth small and free; (3) Legs short, set wide apart, making the waterfowl "waddle"; (4) Dense feathers over a heavy layer of down; (5) Waterfowl moult all of their flight feathers at once, and are flightless for a time each year.

Waterfowl need wetlands. With the draining of these lands for more intensive human use, careful planning is needed to save these birds for the future.

RIVER DUCKS: Sexes different in color; bill broad and flattened; hind toe small, without a lobe or flap; legs near the center of body; feed by "tipping up" mainly on plant food. In taking flight, spring directly up with single bound. (pp. 34-57)

SEA DUCKS: Sexes different in color; bill broad and flattened; hind toe with flap or lobe. Feed by diving after fish, shellfish, and some marine plants. In taking flight they run along water. Legs short, set well back on body. Excellent swimmers. (pp. 58-82)

Mallard   Goldeneye

CANADA GOOSE is the best known and most widely distributed of our waterfowl. There are few places where one or another of the five subspecies of this fine bird cannot be seen at some season. These are the Common, Western, and Lesser Canada geese, and the Richardson's and Cackling geese, all similarly marked and varying principally in size and darkness of coloration.

Flocks migrating north are hailed as harbingers of spring and going south as prophets of winter. On shorter flights to and from feeding grounds the flocks seldom assume the well-known V-shape of migration flight, but move in irregular groups. Many small flocks are families, for geese mate for life and family ties are strong. The old gander usually leads on migration and is believed to teach the young the route.

Most of these geese nest on the ground, but occasionally nest on cliffs. The female incubates the five or six dull, creamy white eggs. The gander stands by for protection and helps rear the brood. Canada Geese are known for their intelligence and often hide to avoid detection. They feed on land, grazing on young plants and picking up waste grain. Their size and wariness have made them a prime favorite with sportsmen.

CANADA GOOSE SUBSPECIES

Western
33-35 in.

Richardson's
22-29 in.

Cackling
22-27 in.

Local Names: Honker, Bay Goose, Black-necked Goose, Ring-neck

Scientific name: *Branta canadensis*

Weights:

	Average		Record	
	lb.	oz.	lb.	oz.
Common: Male	8	7	13	12
Female	7	5	13	0
Lesser: Male	5	12	10	8
Female	5	8	8	8
Cackling: Male	3	6	5	9
Female	2	15	5	1

Sizes:
Common: 32-40 in. Lesser: 26-30 in.

Flight Speeds: Chased: 60 mph
Cruising: 20-45 mph

GEESE 23

AMERICAN BRANT, a true salt-water goose, is seldom found away from the sea. On our shores, most winter from New Jersey south to the North Carolina sounds. The brant is a small goose, not much larger than a Mallard. Its black head and neck with a white collar, broken before and behind, are distinctive. This and the sharp break between the dark neck and light belly aid identification. In winter this goose feeds mainly on eel grass, which grows in tidal water. Some years ago disease almost destroyed the eel grass beds and with them the brant. Recently the eel grass has started to recover and brant are on the increase. Brant nest along the Arctic coast where three to five eggs are deposited in a well-made nest. The female alone incubates but the the male helps raise the young. They fly in long lines low over the water, abreast or in irregular bunches, with no well-defined leader.

Local names: Black Brant	**Weights:**	Average		Record	
Scientific name: *Branta bernicla*		lb.	oz.	lb.	oz.
Size: 24 in.	Male	3	5	4	0
Flight speeds: 45 mph	Female	2	12	3	11

BLACK BRANT, the Pacific coast species, is much like the American Brant and, like it, prefers salt bays and estuaries. It is darker, the black of the head and neck shading into the dark breast below. A flight of these small geese is fascinating to watch. They fly swiftly, low over the water, abreast in line. From time to time they all shift direction for a moment and then swing back on course. This maneuver is often accompanied by a change of elevation, giving the line a rising and falling pattern. The Pacific coast eel grass suffered no loss from disease so the population of Black Brant is still quite good.

Local names: China Goose, Eskimo Goose, Sea Brant
Scientific name: *Branta nigricans*

Weights:	Average		Record	
	lb.	oz.	lb.	oz.
Male	3	7	4	14
Female	3	0	3	10

Size: 23-29 in.
Flight speeds: 45 mph

American Brant

Black Brant

WHITE-FRONTED GEESE, known more commonly as Specklebellies, are primarily western birds, rare on the East Coast. Recognize them by the spotted or splotched black and white belly which gives them their common name. The central valley of California and the coasts of Texas and Louisiana are the principal wintering areas of this goose. Here at times they are abundant. They are found in Europe and Asia as well as in North America. Like most geese, the White-fronts breed in the Arctic. Nests are depressions in the tundra lined with down, dried grass and leaves. The five or six eggs take about a month to hatch into small yellow goslings. September often finds these geese on their wintering grounds, as they are one of the first to migrate. They fly high, often in V's like Canada Geese, and can be mistaken for them at long range. Their call is a loud laughing *wah-wah-wah* which has given these birds another local name, Laughing Goose. White-fronted Geese prefer plant food. They spend much of their time grazing on young shoots and waste grains of wheat, rice and barley. In one part of the Sacramento Valley a larger, darker, white-fronted goose has been described and named the Tule Goose. It is said to prefer willow-lined sloughs and beds of tules (cattail) rather than the open country preferred by its smaller kin. The nesting grounds of the Tule Goose, far up in the Arctic on a tributary of the Perry River, were not discovered until the summer of 1941.

juvenile

adult

Tule Goose

Local names: Specklebelly, Gray Wavy, Brant, Laughing Goose
Scientific name: *Anser albifrons*

Weights:

	Average		Record	
	lb.	oz.	lb.	oz.
White-front:				
Male	5	5	7	5
Female	4	14	6	8
Tule:				
Male	6	10	7	8
Female	5	12	6	8

Size: 27-30 in.
Flight speeds: No information

GEESE 27

SNOW GEESE (two well-defined subspecies) are probably the most abundant of our geese. The most common is the Lesser Snow Goose, a bird of the Mississippi Valley and the West. In past years almost incredible numbers were found in California and on the Texas coast. But, like many species, it was sadly reduced. However, great flocks are still seen, possibly due in some degree to the less desirable table qualities of this bird.

Snows fly in long diagonal lines and curves, and sometimes in V's. While on the wing and much of the time on the ground they keep up a steady chorus of high pitched, shrill cries. The Arctic coast is their nesting ground. Four to eight eggs are laid in early June.

The Greater Snow Goose is found on the Atlantic coast and is much less common than its western relative. All of them winter in a rather restricted part of the coast from Maryland to North Carolina. It is a larger and chunkier bird than the Lesser Snow Goose.

The rare Ross' Goose, looking like a miniature Snow Goose, is just about the size of a Mallard. These tiny geese all winter in a small part of the Sacramento Valley, where they are rigidly protected. Their small size and silence on the wing set them apart from the Snows.

Snow Goose

bill

Ross' Goose

bill

juvenile

Local names: Brant, White Brant,
White Wavy
Scientific name: *Chen hyperborea*
Weights:

	Average		Record	
	lb.	oz.	lb.	oz.
Greater:				
Male	7	4	10	7
Female	6	2	6	8
Lesser:				
Male	5	4	6	12
Female	4	11	5	9

Size: 23-38 in.
Flight speeds: Chased: 50 mph

GEESE 29

BLUE GOOSE is the most distinctive North American goose. Its white head and dark body set it apart instantly. Years ago it was a bird of mystery and was thought rare until its main wintering grounds on the coast of Louisiana were found. Blue Geese are sometimes fantastically abundant there — in a narrow strip from the delta of the Mississippi River to near Vermilion Bay. They occur east and west of this zone only as stragglers. It was not until 1929 that their Arctic breeding grounds were discovered on Baffin and Southampton Islands. On migrations Blue Geese move in large flocks and, in the fall, with large numbers of Snow Geese, they congregate in James Bay before moving south. In habits the Blue Goose is like the Snow Goose, and the two are considered by some authorities to be color phases of a single species. Hybrids occur regularly. These show white on the body, usually on the belly. Blue Geese feed mainly on the roots of sedges, grasses, and cattails. They feed in dense flocks, each bird digging a small hole and eating roots as found until a meadow or low pasture is reduced to a shallow, muddy pool. Blue Geese are noisy birds and on the wintering grounds there is a constant sound like that of distant surf.

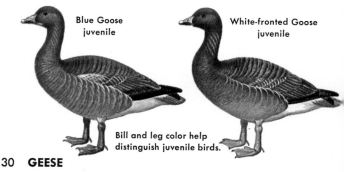

Blue Goose
juvenile

White-fronted Goose
juvenile

Bill and leg color help
distinguish juvenile birds.

juvenile

Local names: Brant, Blue Brant, Blue Wavy

Scientific name: *Chen caerulescens*

Weights:

	Average		Record	
	lb.	oz.	lb.	oz.
Male	5	8	7	8
Female	4	13	6	4

Size: 25-30 in.

Flight speeds: Probably similar to Snow Goose

GEESE 31

EMPEROR GOOSE has been seen by fewer people than any other goose. This is too bad, as it is one of the most attractive geese. A maritime bird, it spends its life within a few miles of the coast. Most Emperors breed in northern Alaska. The Eskimos of that region take many for food. Even in winter it is a bird of the north, living in the Aleutian Islands and on the southwest coast of Alaska. Only stragglers reach the shores of Washington, Oregon and California. The food of this goose is principally mussels and other shellfish, giving the flesh a strong odor and stronger flavor.

Local names:	Beach Goose, Painted Goose			
Scientific name:	*Philacte canagica*			
Weights:	Average		Record	
	lb.	oz.	lb.	oz.
Male	6	10	6	12
Female	6	1	6	14
Size: 26 in.				
Flight speeds:	No information			

FULVOUS TREE DUCK represents a tropical family which finds its way into the S.W. Tree ducks are goose-like in posture and, like geese, the males and females are similar. They moult only once a year. The Fulvous Tree Duck is easily identified by its long neck, legs projecting beyond tail when in flight, and by its tawny-brown color. Another tree duck, the Black-bellied (p. 19), occasionally enters south Texas. Tree ducks nest in high grasses along marshes. The nests, which lack a lining of down, contain 12-17 white, roundish eggs. Tree ducks feed on grass and weed seeds, rice, alfalfa and acorns.

Local names: Mexican Squealer, Squealer, Long-legged Duck
Scientific name: *Dendrocygna bicolor*

Weights:

	Average		Record	
	lb.	oz.	lb.	oz.
Male	1	11	1	14
Female	1	10	1	15

Size: 20-21 in.
Flight speeds: No information

TREE DUCKS 33

MALLARDS introduce the subfamily of river and pond, or surface ducks (p. 21). Mallards are the most important ducks to man, being the ancestor of nearly all domestic forms which are prized for their feathers, flesh, and eggs. Mallards live throughout the Northern Hemisphere but are less common in eastern U.S., being replaced there by their close relative, the Black Duck. Mallards winter mainly in the lower Mississippi Valley and Gulf Coast, moving north as ice melts. Most of their breeding ground is in Canada.

For identification note the male's yellow bill, green head, and neck with a white ring. The female is a streaked, mottled buff-brown. Look for the white borders on the blue wing patches. Males moult in summer and develop plumage like the females. Then, in fall, a second moult produces the striking pattern of breeding plumage.

Mallards feed mainly on water and marsh plants, occasionally taking grain, larger seeds, hickory nuts and acorns. They nest on fairly dry ground, usually near water, but occasionally in trees. Females lay 8 to 10 eggs, incubating them for about 26 days. The female alone cares for the yellow-and-black, downy young. The males go off and gather in small flocks. Mallards are large ducks, excellent eating, and prized by hunters. Many hybrids with other ducks are known. (See page 44.)

Mallard

COMPARISON OF WINGS

Black Duck

Mottled Duck

Male in early fall.

Male in late fall.

Local names: Greenhead, English
Duck, Wild Duck, Stock Duck
Scientific name: *Anas platyrhyn-
chos*

Weights:	Average		Record	
	lb.	oz.	lb.	oz.
Male	2	11	4	4
Female	2	5	3	10

Size: 20-28 in.
Flight speeds: Cruising: 30 mph
Chased: 40-50 mph

RIVER DUCKS 35

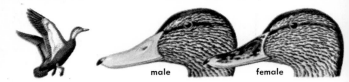

male   female

BLACK DUCK, close relative of the Mallard, is smaller, faster, and much more common in the East where it outnumbers all other river ducks. It is a strong flier, wary and hard to decoy. A Black Duck takes off from the water in an 8 ft. leap; may dive when pressed. In flight the white lining of the wings helps identification. Closer, note the

BREAST FEATHERS

male

female

juvenile

mottled brown color (not black despite its name). The metallic blue speculum on the wings lacks a white border. The older name of Dusky Duck is more descriptive of the bird. Male and female are similar. Note differences in breast feathers illustrated to the left.

Black Ducks nest along the middle Atlantic seaboard, north and west through the Great Lakes, and up through Newfoundland. The nest is well concealed, usually on the ground near water. Small islands with thick vegetation are favorite nest sites. Eight to 12 eggs are laid and cared for by the female. Black Ducks take more animal food, especially mollusks and insects, than Mallards. Plant food is mainly water plants. Black Ducks are more often found in salt marshes and near salt water than other river ducks.

In fall Black Ducks migrate early, wintering all through the Southeast. Red legged Black Ducks are not a subspecies, as previously thought, but merely older individuals, usually larger and with red feet.

Local names: Redleg, Black Mallard, Blackie

Scientific name: *Anas rubripes*

Weights:

	Average		Record	
	lb.	oz.	lb.	oz.
Male	2	11	3	12
Female	2	6	3	4

Size: 21-25 in.

Flight speeds: Cruising: 26 mph

MEXICAN DUCK (New Mexican Duck) is limited to a restricted S.W. area, but even here it is easily confused with the female Mallard, being only slightly darker in color and with a brighter bill (see below). Mexican Ducks live along the upper Rio Grande on bars and mudflats. They are shy, wary birds, stronger and faster in flight than Mallards, with which they are often seen. Mexican Ducks feed on water and marsh plants. At night they venture into irrigated fields of grain. No weight or flight speed data is available.

COMPARISON OF BILLS

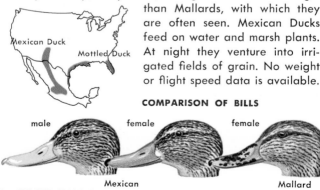

male   female   female

Mexican   Mallard

MOTTLED DUCK lives only along the Gulf and in Florida. Here it is more common than Black Ducks, with which it is often found. The Mottled Duck is lighter in color with greater contrast between the head and the body. Its yellow bill does *not* have dark patches, as does the female Mallard's. In this respect it is like the Mexican Duck (p. 38). It does not migrate and is less shy than the Black Duck.

The Mottled Duck is also called the Florida or Summer Mallard. Once the Florida form was considered a separate species—the Florida Duck. The Mottled Duck nests in high grass near the water, laying 8 to 10 eggs which the female alone cares for. These ducks eat much animal food—mollusks and insects. Flight speed and weights are probably similar to Blacks'.

BREAST FEATHERS

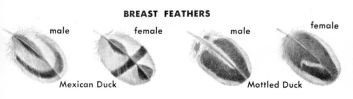

male   female   male   female

Mexican Duck   Mottled Duck

GADWALL ranges the world over except in South America and Australia, yet it is not a very common bird. In North America it is more abundant in the central plains and the West, though it winters in the South and Southeast. The Gadwall has few good field marks for identification. The male is gray, black around the tail, and has much white in the wing speculum. The female is browner and similar to Pintails and Widgeon. Gadwalls move south late in the fall and return north early in the spring. They travel in small flocks, often with Pintails and Widgeon. The Gadwall is not especially prized as a gamebird, yet it is good eating. Its food is almost entirely vegetable (98% in fall and winter) and includes much pondweed, sedge and bulrush. Gadwalls occasionally feed in grain fields. They dive for food more than other pond ducks. They also walk well, and search for grain far from their ponds. They nest in high grass, sometimes quite far from water, though islands seem preferred. Ten to 12 white eggs are laid. When the young ducks hatch, they feed mainly on small water insects. The principal nesting area is shown on the range map. Both the male and the female have a loud quack which is higher in tone than that of the female Mallard.

COMPARISON OF FEMALES

Gadwall   Pintail   American Widgeon

male

female

wing of male

wing of female

Local names: Gray Duck, Gaddy, Gray Widgeon
Scientific name: *Anas strepera*
Weights:

	Average		Record	
	lb.	oz.	lb.	oz.
Male	2	0	2	10
Female	1	13	3	0

Size: 19-21 in.
Flight speeds: Cruising: 29 mph

RIVER DUCKS 41

AMERICAN WIDGEON, or Baldpate, breeds and usually winters on this continent, though a few continue to the West Indies and northern S. America. In flight both the male and female show a white patch on the forewing. Otherwise the female is similar to the female Gadwall (p. 40) but has pinker sides and a whiter breast. Note the male's white crown, pinkish sides, and the white spot near the tail. Widgeon are alert, nervous birds and often warn other ducks of danger when feeding. They fly in small, compact flocks, moving rapidly and directly. In mid-spring they start north towards breeding grounds among inland ponds and swamps, though the nest itself may not be close to water. In it 9 to 11 creamy white eggs are laid. While the male stays around until the moulting season, it does not care for the young. Because Widgeon come north late, they are among the last ducks to complete egg laying. The young hatch in 24 to 25 days.

Widgeon feed in shallow water. They also graze like geese in fields of grain or alfalfa. Roots of water celery and other deep water plants are relished; they often steal these from diving ducks. This habit gives them the local name of "Poacher." Widgeon move quickly and keep hunters alert. They are not a preferred table bird.

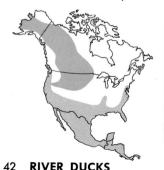

Local names: Baldpate, Widgeon, Blue-billed Widgeon, Whistler, Poacher
Scientific name: *Mareca americana*
Weights:

	Average		Record	
	lb.	oz.	lb.	oz.
Male	1	11	2	8
Female	1	8	1	14

Size: 18-22 in.
Flight speeds: Cruising: 22 mph

American Widgeon

male

female

EUROPEAN WIDGEON, below, is a visitor to coastal states. It rarely goes inland. Note the male's rust-red head, creamy crown, and gray body, in contrast to the overall brown of the male American Widgeon. Female is similar to American species but head is more reddish. The European Widgeon is locally called a Redhead Widgeon. Weights run slightly less than the American Widgeon.

female

male

European Widgeon

PINTAILS are rated, after Mallards and Black Ducks, as the third most popular waterfowl. They are excellent hunting and equally good eating. Their long, thin shape identifies both male and female in the air. When the male is swimming, its thin tail is also conspicuous. Pintails are fast, high fliers, dropping into a feeding area with a steep rush. Pintails have the widest breeding distribution of any river duck. They breed over a large area in the N.W.—also in northern Europe and Asia—and winter along all our coasts except in New England. Pintails move north soon after the lakes are free of ice. Birds pair off en route and are ready to nest early. Less than ten eggs are laid and tended by the female. The male stands by until he goes off to moult. In fall Pintails move south early and, especially in California, feed in grain fields on the way, occasionally becoming a problem to farmers.

Pintails feed by "tipping up" in typical river duck fashion, but they have the advantage of longer necks. Food is mainly water plants and seeds—bulrush, smartweed and pondweed preferred. Mollusks and insects make up the animal food. The voice of the male Pintail is a low mellow whistle; that of the female a low quack.

BAHAMA DUCK of the West Indies is a small bird (15-18 inches), male and female similar. Note the white cheek and throat. Overshooting has depleted this handsome species.

MALLARD HYBRID is only one of many natural crosses involving Mallards (p. 34) and others. Note the Mallard head color and the sharp but up-curved tail, combining characteristics of both Pintail and Mallard.

44 **RIVER DUCKS**

female

male

Local names: Sprig, Sprig-tail, Longneck, Gray Duck (female)

Scientific name: *Anas acuta*

Weights:

	Average		Record	
	lb.	oz.	lb.	oz.
Male	2	3	3	7
Female	1	13	2	6

Size: 26-30 in.

Flight speeds: Chased: 65 mph

RIVER DUCKS 45

 GREEN-WINGED TEAL is the smallest and one of the most beautiful waterfowl. The dark red head and white crescent in front of the shoulder identify the male. Teal fly swiftly and erratically. Their small size and quick getaway make their speed seem even greater than it is. Teal come in a dense flock, wheeling and turning in unison like a band of sandpipers. This flight pattern is characteristic.

Green-winged Teal move north very early in spring to nesting grounds in the northern prairies and in western Canada. The nest is in high grass, usually near water. Ten

Green-winged Teal
male

Common Teal
male

male

female

to 12 eggs are laid, occasionally as many as 18. The male deserts the female soon after the eggs are laid.

Green-winged Teal are primarily plant-eaters, making wide use of seeds of bulrush, pondweed and panic grass. Animal food includes insects and mollusks. In turn, they are excellent eating and are favorites of hunters. They respond to decoys and circle an area even during firing.

The Common Teal, similar to the Green-winged, lacks the white crescent on the wing but has a horizontal white bar. This Eurasian bird occasionally visits our Northwest and East coast. It is more common in the Aleutians.

Local names: Common Teal, Teal, Butterball, Red-head Teal
Scientific name: *Anas carolinensis*

Weights:	Average		Record	
	lb.	oz.	lb.	oz.
Male	0	13	1	0
Female	0	11	0	15

Size: 13-15 in.
Flight speeds: Cruising: 30 mph
Chased: 40 mph

BLUE-WINGED TEAL is, like its relatives, a small, plump, speedy duck, as widely known and as admired by hunters. The Blue-wing is a bird of the New World (other teal range into Europe and Asia). It is most common in the eastern and central part of the continent and occurs but rarely on the Pacific coast. In winter the Blue-wings go farther south than any other North American duck. They are common in Mexico, where they are widely hunted, and some go as far as Brazil and Chile. Their northern migration begins late in the spring and reaches its peak after other waterfowl have moved on. The nesting grounds of the Blue-winged Teal are in the ponds, marshes and potholes of the northern plains of the U.S. and Canada. The actual land available for nesting has been cut down by agriculture and drainage of swamps. However, the establishment of refuge areas now helps preserve the teal population. The nest, well lined with down, is in tall grass near the water. The female lays 10 to 12 cream or light olive eggs which hatch in about 21 days. She alone cares for the eggs and young.

Fall migration begins early. Often the older males move south separately. Late nesting tends to delay the departure of the young, though they grow and mature rapidly. Later flights are mainly young and females. Blue-wings migrate leisurely, lingering at ponds to feed. Blue-wings prefer to feed in very shallow water and hence make more use of farm ponds than other ducks. They take more animal food (mainly mollusks and water insects) than Green-wings, but about 70% of their diet is seeds and soft parts of water plants. Like other teal they are excellent eating and, because they fly in tight flocks and respond readily to decoys, Blue-wings make good targets for hunters. The voices of both male and female are weak.

male

female

Local names: Teal, Blue Teal, Summer Teal

Scientific name: *Anas discors*

Weights:

	Average		Record	
	lb.	oz.	lb.	oz.
Male	0	14	1	4
Female	0	13	1	3

Size: 15-16 in.

Flight speeds: Probably the same as other teal—cruising, 30-40 mph; chased, up to 50 mph.

RIVER DUCKS 49

CINNAMON TEAL is the only river duck with a range limited to the area west of the Rocky Mts. Another group of these ducks live in S. America but have no migrations or other connections to the N. American group. The male, with its cinnamon-red color, cannot be mistaken, but the drab female is almost identical with the female Blue-wing except that the bill is longer. Migration is simple; it consists only of withdrawal from the northern part of the range in fall. Over most of its range the Cinnamon Teal is a permanent resident. The nest, of down-lined grass, is placed near the water. Unlike other ducks, however, the male stays nearby and helps rear the young. The female lays 6 to 14 eggs and incubates them alone. The small flocks seen in the fall are usually family groups. Large flocks are rare. Southern birds move north in March and April.

Cinnamon Teal feed in very shallow water or on banks of ponds and sloughs. Most of their food is bulrush, pond-weed, saltgrass and sedge—both seeds and soft parts. Insects and mollusks are the principal animal food. These ducks are an important game species over all their range. Their flight habits are similar to other teal.

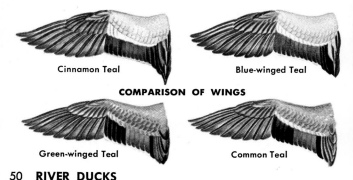

Cinnamon Teal

Blue-winged Teal

COMPARISON OF WINGS

Green-winged Teal

Common Teal

male

female

Local names:	Blue-wing, Red Teal, River Teal			
Scientific name:	*Anas cyanoptera*			
Weights:	Average		Record	
	lb.	oz.	lb.	oz.
Male	0	13	1	3
Female	0	13	1	2
Size:	15-17 in.			
Flight speeds:	Cruising: 33 mph			
	Chased: 50 mph			

SHOVELLER, named for its huge, spoon-shaped bill, is a well-known and widely distributed duck. It is found throughout the Northern Hemisphere and has close relatives in the Southern. Except for its bill, the female Shoveller is nondescript—mottled brown with some blue on the wing. The male is bright and distinctively marked, showing more white than any other river duck. Shovellers are closely related to teal and resemble them in flight, but usually fly more slowly and directly. They have the same wing pattern as Blue-wings. Shovellers move north late in spring and head south early in fall. On the southward move, Shovellers often fly with Blue-wings but, when moving north, they tend to stay in small flocks by themselves. On the breeding grounds a female Shoveller is often accompanied by two or more males. She nests near a pond or slough and lays 6 to 14 pale olive-buff eggs. Newly-hatched young have normally proportioned bills, but within two weeks the distinctive size and shape are evident. Meanwhile, the males have left to form small summer flocks. Shovellers are surface feeders. They swim slowly, low in the water, with bills pointed downward. As food they take seeds and soft parts of water plants; also, more small animal life than other ducks. They strain larvae of water insects and small crustaceans out of the mud with the unusually well-developed, comb-like "teeth" in their bills. Shovellers respond to decoys but their flesh has a poor flavor and texture.

DETAILS OF BILL

side   top

Lamellae or comb-like "teeth"

female

male

Local names: Spoony, Spoon-bill,
Broad-bill, Shovel-bill
Scientific name: _Spatula clypeata_

Weights:	Average		Record	
	lb.	oz.	lb.	oz.
Male	1	7	2	0
Female	1	4	1	10

Size: 17-20 in.
Flight speeds: Cruising: 25 mph
Chased: 50 mph

RIVER DUCKS 53

WOOD DUCK, praised as the most handsome waterfowl, is a medium-sized bird of wooded river bottoms and forested streams. Wood Ducks fly rapidly through the trees, twisting and dodging with great agility. In flight they hold their heads high with bills pointed down. This position, and the duck's long dark tail make both sexes easy to identify. There are two populations of Wood Ducks in the U.S., one in the East and the other in the N.W. These do not mix but both migrate, moving south in their range during winter. Wood Ducks lay their eggs in trees—in a natural cavity or in the abandoned hole of a large woodpecker. Eight to 15 small round eggs are laid. They hatch in about 27 days and the downy young, which have sharp claws and a hook nail at the tip of their bill, climb to the entrance of the hole and jump to the ground. They are so light they are not injured by the fall. The Wood Duck diet is mainly vegetable. Wild rice, pondweed, dogwood and acorns are preferred foods, but other seeds, fruits and soft plants are eaten. In spring and early summer some insects are taken, too. Wood Ducks are favorites of sportsmen, hunted not only as food but also as trophies and as a source of feathers for making trout flies. Hunting plus drainage of swamps once depleted the Wood Duck population. Now it is partially restored and limited hunting is permitted. Wood Ducks move well on land and swim rapidly. The typical call, ooo-eek, ooo-eek, is usually given as the birds take off.

DETAIL OF WINGS

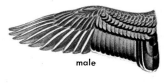

male

female

female

male

Local names: Woody, Summer Duck, Squealer, Tree Duck

Scientific name: *Aix sponsa*

Weights:

	Average		Record	
	lb.	oz.	lb.	oz.
Male	1	9	2	0
Female	1	7	2	0

Size: 17-20 in.

Flight speeds: 30-50 mph

RIVER DUCKS 55

Male

Female

RUDDY DUCKS (and Masked Ducks), in their own subfamily, are unique in many ways. The male Ruddy Duck has two complete plumages, as shown on the next page. The dark crown, white cheeks, stiff tail and chunky shape identify it any time of the year. Ruddys do not rise from the water easily, but patter along for some distance before taking off. Their rapid wing beats give them a fast buzzy flight, usually low over the water. They can sink without diving and use this odd talent as a means of escape. On land they are very awkward. The male carries its tail erect. It has a bright blue bill.

Females lay 6 to 12 eggs which are huge for the birds' size, in a nest hung in thick reeds over the water or even set on a floating log. The male Ruddy, unlike most other ducks, helps to care for the young.

The diet of the Ruddy Duck is mainly seeds and soft parts of water plants. These are secured by diving. In summer, water insects, small mollusks and crustaceans are eaten, too.

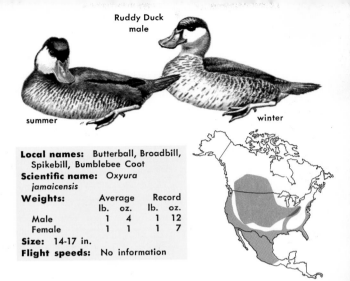

Ruddy Duck
male

summer

winter

Local names: Butterball, Broadbill, Spikebill, Bumblebee Coot
Scientific name: *Oxyura jamaicensis*

Weights:	Average		Record	
	lb.	oz.	lb.	oz.
Male	1	4	1	12
Female	1	1	1	7

Size: 14-17 in.
Flight speeds: No information

MASKED DUCK, below, similar to the Ruddy Duck and related, has a black head, white wing patch, and mottled back. The female is similar to the Ruddy but has two black streaks on its head, and a white wing patch like the male's. The Masked Duck, common in the tropics, occasionally enters the lower Rio Grande Valley of Texas. Its habits are generally like those of the Ruddy Duck.

Masked Duck

female

male

REDHEADS introduce the sea or diving ducks (p. 21), well-known and widely distributed. All have common subfamily features and habits. They occur in all states during some part of the year, spreading out from breeding grounds in south central Canada and north central U.S. Among diving ducks they rank second only to Canvasbacks as a game species. Migrating Redheads fly in V-shaped flocks but on shorter flights they move in bunches or in irregular lines. Their flight is fast and direct. They drop down from great heights with a loud ripping sound of wings. Flocks usually fly both morning and evening. During the day they will flush and settle back at intervals. The well-made nest is placed in cattails or bulrushes near deep water. It may contain 10-15 eggs which the female incubates alone. Females may also lay eggs in any other nearby duck nests. The redhead's diet is 90% vegetable—

a higher percentage than other diving ducks'. Leaves and stems of aquatic plants such as pondweed, wild celery, bulrush and widgeongrass are preferred. Redheads dive for these and also feed in shallows, with river ducks, for water insects, mollusks and snails.

Redheads are endangered because their breeding grounds are in areas suitable for agriculture. With establishment of adequate refuges their future may be made more secure.

female

male

Local names: Fiddler, Red-headed Bluebill

Scientific name: *Aythya americana*

Weights:

	Average lb.	oz.	Record lb.	oz.
Male	2	7	3	0
Female	2	3	3	15

Size: 18-23 in.

Flight speeds: Cruising: 42 mph
Chased: 55 mph

SEA DUCKS 59

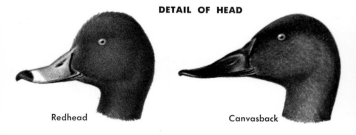

CANVASBACK is the most famous of our waterfowl. It is an epicure's delight and a thrill to the sportsman. Found only in N. America, the Canvasback has been recorded elsewhere only once. Its large size and very white back, set off by dark areas in front and behind, mark it at long range. Both sexes show the characteristic long neck and sloping profile. In flight the Canvasback is swift and direct, using a V-formation on migration. On shorter flights a compact flock is usual. It is hardy and seldom moves southward until after a hard freeze. It winters in large numbers in Middle Atlantic bays and estuaries. In spring it moves north with the first breaks in the ice. Canvasbacks breed mainly in prairie regions of central Canada. Here they nest in sloughs and ponds among cattails and rushes. Females incubate 7 to 9 eggs alone. Males gather in flocks on open water during the moult. Nearly 80% of the Canvasback's food is vegetable. Wild celery (*Vallisneria*) is most important but pondweed, foxtail grass and others are used. The animal portion of the diet is primarily snails and crustaceans. The Canvasback is sought-after because of its fame as a table bird. This, coupled with drainage of areas in its breeding grounds, has made hunting restrictions necessary.

DETAIL OF HEAD

Redhead   Canvasback

male

female

Local names:	Can, Bullneck			
Scientific name:	*Aythya valisineria*			
Weights:		Average		Record
		lb.	oz.	lb.	oz.
Male		2	12	3	8
Female		2	9	3	7
Size: 20-24 in.				
Flight speeds: Chased: 72 mph				

RING-NECKED DUCK is rather unfortunately named as the ring is quite inconspicuous. It might better have been called the Ring-billed Duck from the easily seen white band on its dark bill. The males are black on the back and show a vertical white bar in front of the wing. Females are similar to female Redheads but are smaller and show the ring on the bill. In flight Ring-necks lack the flashy white wing patches of the closely related scaups. They move in small flocks, flying fast and straight, rising from the water more easily than other diving ducks. Ring-necks often migrate with scaups or in small groups by themselves.

The nest, containing 8 to 12 eggs, is built over water or on the edge of a pond. One favorite site is a grassy tussock in the water. The male does not help care for the young. Ring-necks are primarily vegetarians. About 80% of what they eat consists of leaves of pondweeds, bulbs of water lilies, seeds of grasses, and other plant material. Insects and snails make up most of their animal food. They feed in shallow water but dive well when necessary, feeding to a depth of 40 ft. Woodland swamps, ponds and streams are favored winter habitats. Ring-necks drop into decoys readily. However, their fast flight and loose flocks make them a difficult target for sportsmen. They are usually fine table ducks.

Ring-necked Duck female

Greater Scaup female

Lesser Scaup female

female

male

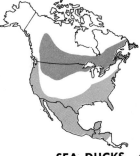

Local names: Blackjack, Ringbill,
Pond Bluebill
Scientific name: *Aythya collaris*

Weights:	Average		Record	
	lb.	oz.	lb.	oz.
Male	1	10	2	6
Female	1	10	2	0

Size: 16-18 in.
Flight speeds: No information

Greater Scaup

female

male

GREATER and **LESSER SCAUPS** are difficult to distinguish. The Greater averages only ¼ lb. heavier. It has a greenish gloss on its head; the Lesser has purple. In flight the Greater shows more white on the wing. It prefers larger lakes and rivers, and winters on the seacoast. The Lesser prefers smaller ponds and marshes in both summer and winter. The Greater breeds and winters to the north of the Lesser. Both fly fast and in tight formations, with the Lesser more erratic and lively in its flight. Both species nest on the ground near water. The 7 to 12 eggs are incubated only by the female, which is not easily flushed from the nest. Males gather in open water during their moult.

Both scaups take about half plant and half animal food in their diet. Seeds, roots and leaves of aquatic plants are preferred plant foods; mollusks make up most of the ani-

COMPARISON OF WINGS

Greater Scaup

Lesser Scaup

Lesser Scaup

female

male

mal food. Both are good divers and can remain long under water. They decoy well and are important game species. When alarmed they give a loud raucous *scaup*.

During local flights around the feeding grounds, scaups stay close to the water, but during migrations they fly high.

Recent studies indicate that the breeding range of the Greater Scaup is more limited in North America than previously supposed. The Lesser Scaup has a wide breeding range in North America, but its range does not extend into the Old World as does the Greater Scaup's. Both species form large dense flocks on water in the winter, giving them the local name of "raft ducks."

Local names: Blackhead, Bluebill, Broadbill
Scientific names:
  Greater Scaup: *Aythya marila*
  Lesser Scaup: *Aythya affinis*

Weights:	Average		Record	
	lb.	oz.	lb.	oz.
Greater: Male	2	3	2	14
Female	2	0	2	15
Lesser: Male	1	13	2	8
Female	1	11	2	2

Size: Greater: 17-20 in.
  Lesser: 15-18 in.
Flight speeds: No information

Greater Scaup

Lesser Scaup

COMMON GOLDENEYE is often called "Whistler" because of the loud, penetrating sounds of its wings in flight. Widely distributed in North America, it has a close relative in Europe and Asia. The male shows much white, both on the water and in flight. This, with the white face patch on the black head, makes identification easy. The female has a gray body and a rich brown head. Goldeneye is a hardy species, wintering as far north as open water may be found. Many are seen in the Great Lakes during winter but more prefer the seacoasts. When migrating, Goldeneyes move in comparatively small flocks at high altitudes.

The Goldeneye nest is placed in a tree cavity or on top of a rotted stump near water. In it 8 to 12 eggs are laid and covered with a dense layer of down. When about two days old the young jump safely from this unusual duck nest. Old tales of the female carrying out her young have proved to be false. For food the Goldeneye takes about 75% animal matter—crustaceans, insects, and mollusks. It is an expert diver and is said to overturn rocks under water when searching for food.

The Goldeneye is a wary bird and is decoyed with difficulty. They are not considered good table ducks but hunters like them because of their shyness and swift, erratic flight. They are one of the most common ducks and are widely distributed. Goldeneyes are noisy birds, especially in the spring.

female

male

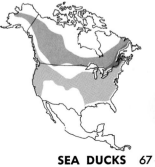

Local names: Whistler, Tree Duck, Wood Duck, Copperhead (female)
Scientific name: *Bucephala clangula*

Weights:

	Average		Record	
	lb.	oz.	lb.	oz.
Male	2	3	3	1
Female	1	12	2	8

Size: 17-23 in.
Flight speeds: Cruising: about 50 mph

SEA DUCKS 67

female

male

BARROW'S GOLDENEYE has both an eastern and western population, the latter involving breeding grounds high in the Rocky Mountains. Here it prefers fast mountain streams. Very similar to the previous Goldeneye, it is distinguished by the head shape and, in the males, by the crescent-shaped face patch. Females of the two species are almost impossible to distinguish in the field. Migrations involve only a short movement south, usually in small flocks, and a shift to more open feeding grounds. Barrow's Goldeneye also nests in trees and may also nest as far as half-a-mile from water. Its food is about 75% animal matter, and this makes it less favored as a game species. All Goldeneyes are noisy ducks.

Local names: Whistler, Rocky Mountain Goldeneye
Scientific name: *Bucephala islandica*

Weights:	Average		Record	
	lb.	oz.	lb.	oz.
Male	2	7	2	14
Female	1	10	1	14

Size: 20-23 in.
Flight speeds: No information

male
female

Female at
nesting hole

BUFFLEHEAD is the smallest diving duck. Its small size, large head, and white head patch identify both sexes. Buffleheads are found in small flocks of young birds, females, and one or two old males. They fly fast and, unlike other diving ducks, rise directly from the surface. Migration is in late fall and many move only as far south as forced to by the ice. Most winter along the coast and are among the last ducks to go north in spring. Buffleheads are also tree-nesting ducks, using the holes made by large woodpeckers in trees near the water. Ten to 12 eggs are laid on the floor of the cavity. Bufflehead diet is about 80% animal. These ducks come to decoys readily but few are shot by hunters because they are poor eating.

Local names:	Butterball, Dipper, Spirit Duck			
Scientific name:	*Bucephala albeola*			
Weights:	Average		Record	
	lb.	oz.	lb.	oz.
Male	1	0	1	4
Female	0	11	1	5
Size: 13-15 in.				
Flight speeds:	Cruising: 48 mph			

SEA DUCKS 69

summer
male
female

OLDSQUAW is a maritime duck, breeding on the cold circumpolar coasts. It is one of the few ducks with two complete annual plumage changes. Identify the male by its small size, chunky shape and long tail. The dark pied brown and white head of the female is distinctive. In flight note the nearly white body (both male and female) and the male's long tail. The flight is swift and low with many twists and turns. Oldsquaws rise from the water quickly. They nest on the tundra, often quite far from water, laying 5 to 7 eggs in a down-filled nest.

Oldsquaws are champion divers with a record of 180 feet. Their diet is about 90% animal food.

winter
male
female

Local name: Long-tailed Duck
Scientific name: *Clangula hyemalis*

Weights:

	Average		Record	
	lb.	oz.	lb.	oz.
Male	1	13	2	5
Female	1	7	1	12

Size: Male, 21 in. Female, 16 in.
Flight speeds: No information

female

male

HARLEQUIN DUCKS are birds of rough, rocky coasts and rushing streams. The small, dark males have oddly placed white markings and reddish-brown sides. Note the female's chunky shape and the three white spots on its head. Two populations of Harlequin Ducks, Atlantic and Pacific, spend most of their lives on the ocean, moving into the interior to breed. Their flight is swift and direct, but when following a stream they follow every twist and turn. The nest is usually on the ground, close to a rapid stream. The female incubates 6 to 7 eggs while the male returns to sea. The Harlequin's diet is practically all animal food—crustaceans, mollusks, and insects. They are not good game and are seldom shot.

Local names: Painted Duck, Lords and Ladies, Rock Duck
Scientific name: *Histrionicus histrionicus*

Weights:	Average		Record	
	lb.	oz.	lb.	oz.
Male	1	8	1	9
Female	1	4	1	5

Size: 15-17-in.
Flight speeds: No information

WHITE-WINGED SCOTER, a bird of the interior in summer and of the seacoast in winter, is the largest North American scoter. Both male and female are heavy bodied, with a characteristic white wing patch. Note the swollen bill and the male's white eye patch. White-wings are more abundant than other scoters but nowhere are they very common during the breeding season. They are similar to and closely related to the Velvet Scoter of Europe.

White-wings have difficulty in taking off for flight and run along the surface for a distance. Once airborne, their flight is strong and swift. In migration, most follow the coast, flying high unless forced down by bad weather. White-wings are late nesters, seldom starting north until the end of June. The nest is hollowed out on high ground, and lined with sticks, leaves and down. In it 9 to 14 eggs are laid. This scoter lives mainly on marine animals, with mollusks making up 94% of its diet. Mussels, scallops and oysters are crushed and dissolved in the birds' powerful gizzards.

Off the New England coast "coot" hunting has been an important sport for many years. Birds are hunted at sea from anchored dories. Shooting is popular despite the poor table qualities of scoters and the rugged hunting conditions. They are seldom taken in other regions.

DETAIL OF WING AND BILL

male

female

male

Local names: Coot, White-wing Coot, Brant Coot

Scientific name: *Melanitta deglandi*

Weights:

	Average lb. oz.	Record lb. oz.
Male	3 8	4 1
Female	2 13	3 3

Size: 20-23 in.

Flight speeds: No information

SEA DUCKS 73

SURF SCOTER is the most widely distributed and best known North American scoter. The unmistakable large white head patches of the male give him the local name "Skunkhead." The female has two obscure white spots on the face but lacks the white wing of the White-wing Scoter. Surf Scoters are lighter than the White-wings and have an easier flight. But they, too, have difficulty in rising from the water and prefer to take off into the wind. In flight they are fast and sure. Just before alighting and just after takeoff, their wings whistle loudly. Surf Scoters travel in large flocks with no regular formation. When migrating they tend to follow the coastline where most winter, but a good many winter on the Great Lakes.

The nest is well concealed, usually in a marsh or bog. Five to 9 pale, buffy eggs are laid and incubated by the female. Surf Scoters, like others, dive expertly and use their wings under water. Their name comes from their habit of feeding in the breaking surf where few other birds venture. Their food is 90% animal, mainly mollusks and crustaceans. New England hunters prefer the young of the Surf Scoter for their better table qualities, although they are still far from choice ducks. Scoters are not hunted much elsewhere.

JUVENILE SCOTERS

White-winged
Scoter

Surf
Scoter

American
Scoter

male

female

Local names: Coot, Skunkhead
   Coot, Bald-headed Coot, Bay Coot
Scientific name: *Melanitta perspi-
cillata*

Weights:

	Average		Record	
	lb.	oz.	lb.	oz.
Male	2	3	2	8
Female	1	15	2	8

Size: 18-22 in.
Flight speeds: No information

juvenile

COMMON SCOTER is seldom found away from the coast in both the Old World and the New. The male is the only N.A. duck that is totally black. Its only color is the swollen, yellow base of the bill. The female is a dark, dusky brown, with pale gray, brown-flecked cheeks and chin. Common Scoters closely resemble Surf Scoters, especially females and young. Common Scoters rise from the water with less effort than their relatives. Their flight is swift, with their wings making a loud whistle. In migration they usually fly high except in stormy weather. They migrate earlier than other scoters and follow coastline irregularities. These restless ducks constantly fly about the feeding grounds.

BILLS

Common Scoter

Surf Scoter

male

female

The nest, near water or on an island, is well-concealed. The female lays 6 to 10 eggs and raises the family alone. The young are adept at evading capture, swimming and diving at an early age. Most scoters are silent birds but this species has a melodious, whistling call. Only in New England is it of any importance for game. Animal matter makes up 90% of the Common Scoter's diet. These ducks are a problem at times in oyster and scallop beds, as these are preferred food. Mussels, razor clams, marine crustaceans and some fish are also eaten.

Local names: Coot, Black Coot, Butter-bill Coot
Scientific name: *Oidemia nigra*

Weights:

	Average		Record	
	lb.	oz.	lb.	oz.
Male	2	7	2	13
Female	1	13	2	7

Size: 17-21 in.
Flight speeds: No information

COMMON EIDER is the source of the famous eiderdown. Most down is now gathered from European birds, as ruthless slaughter has reduced N.A. eiders. Eiders are important to the Eskimo—their eggs for food, skins for clothing and blankets. Eiders, our largest ducks, frequent Arctic seas and are seldom seen away from salt water. The males' striking black and white pattern and the rich, barred brown of the females make identification easy. Their flight appears labored and heavy, but is actually much faster than it seems. They fly close to the water with head low and bill pointed slightly down. On migration small flocks follow the coast. Common Eiders usually nest in loose colonies, almost always on islands close to salt water. The nest is made of sticks and grass and is lined and covered with down. After the 3 to 6 olive-green eggs are laid, the males desert the females and gather in flocks off the coast. Down is usually removed from the nest twice in commercial gathering. If a bird cannot replace the down it substitutes leaves or grass to cover the eggs. Because of the value of down, eiders should be rigidly protected. Eiders are not good eating. Their diet of mollusks and crustaceans makes their flesh strong and fishy.

COMMON EIDER has three subspecies. Pacific subspecies at left; northern subspecies above; American subspecies on p. 79.

female

male

Local names: Sea Duck, Canvasback
Scientific name: *Somateria mollis-
sima*
Weights:

	Average		Record	
	lb.	oz.	lb.	oz.
Male	4	6	6	3
Female	4	6	5	11

Size: 22-26 in.
Flight speeds: No information

SEA DUCKS 79

female

male

STELLER'S EIDER, the smallest eider, is a little-known duck of the Alaskan and Siberian coasts and is not often found south of the Aleutians. It is quite abundant within its range and occasionally forms huge flocks with other eiders. However, it is more duck-like and has a swifter flight. The chestnut underparts, white head and black throat identify the male. The female is smaller, more trim, and has a conspicuous blue wing speculum. The nests are placed on the tundra, usually near water. Six to 10 eggs are laid and covered with a dark-brown down. Unlike other eiders, the male remains near the nest although he takes no part in rearing the young. The food of Steller's Eider is small marine animals.

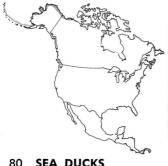

Local names:	None known			
Scientific name:	*Polysticta stelleri*			
Weights:		Average		Record
		lb. oz.		lb. oz.
Male		1 15		2 2
Female		1 15		2 0
Size: 18 in.				
Flight speeds:	No information			

female

male

KING EIDER is found on the Arctic coasts, including northern Europe and Siberia. Even in winter it is an irregular visitor south of Canada. The black back of the male and its large, yellow bill process make it easy to identify. The female is similar to other eider females. King Eiders are quite common off the Alaskan coast and migrate by the thousands. The Aleutians are a favorite wintering area. Kings differ from the Common Eider in nesting on the mainland or on large islands, frequently near ponds or streams. Kings do not form colonies. About 5 eggs are laid. Sea animals make up 95% of their food, and this renders the duck unpalatable. Eskimos are said to relish the fatty knob at the base of the bill.

Local names:	Cousin, Isle-of-Shoals Duck			
Scientific name:	*Somateria spectabilis*			
Weights:	Average		Record	
	lb.	oz.	lb.	oz.
Male	4	0	4	7
Female	3	10	4	2
Size:	21-24 in.			
Flight speeds:	No information			

female

male

SPECTACLED EIDER is one of our least-known water-fowl. A Siberian bird, it breeds only sparingly in Alaska. In winter scattered birds may be found in the Aleutians. Its flight appears rather clumsy, like that of other large eiders. The male looks like the Common Eider but shows the large white eye patch that gives it its name. The female is similar to other eiders but may show a light brown eye patch.

The nest is usually in a grass tussock or on a knoll near a pond. It is a hole in the tundra, lined with down and containing from 5 to 9 eggs. The male leaves the female soon after the eggs are laid. This eider takes more vegetable food than its relatives: 75% of its diet is animal.

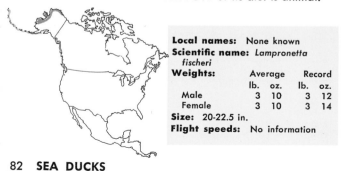

Local names: None known
Scientific name: *Lampronetta fischeri*

Weights:	Average		Record	
	lb.	oz.	lb.	oz.
Male	3	10	3	12
Female	3	10	3	14

Size: 20-22.5 in.
Flight speeds: No information

MERGANSERS or "Fish Ducks" are a Northern Hemisphere group of nine ducks, three of which occur in North America. Most are large, but slim and streamlined for underwater movement. Their bills are long, round in cross section, and have "teeth" for catching and holding fish. Mergansers are sometimes charged with depleting trout and salmon streams. Normally the merganser does not threaten fish populations.

Common   Red Breasted   Hooded

COMMON MERGANSER is our largest merganser. Note its size, dark uncrested head, white chest and sides. The female has a reddish-brown head and well-developed crest. This merganser runs along the surface before taking off. Its flight is fast, usually low over the water, except during migrations when it flies high. The Common Merganser prefers fresh water and is an early spring migrant. It usually nests in a tree cavity or hole in a cliff.

Local names: Goosander, Big Sawbill, Fish Duck, American Merganser
Scientific name: *Mergus merganser*

Weights:

	Average lb.	Average oz.	Record lb.	Record oz.
Male	3	8	4	2
Female	2	12	3	14

Size: 22-27 in.
Flight speeds: No information

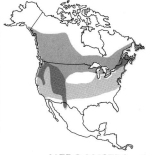

Red-breasted
female

Common
male

Common
female

RED-BREASTED MERGANSER is similar but smaller.
Both male and female show a ragged crest. The male has
a brown chest band. The female Common and Red-
breasted are much alike. In the Common the brown head
is sharply divided from the white chest. In the Red-
breasted the colors run together. The Red-breasted prefers salt water and is found farther south in winter. The
nest is always on the ground. The female usually lays 8
to 10 eggs which she incubates 26 to 28 days. The male
helps care for the young.

Local names: Hairy-head, Salt-
water Shelldrake, Fish Duck
Scientific name: *Mergus serrator*
Weights:

	Average		Record	
	lb.	oz.	lb.	oz.
Male	2	10	2	14
Female	2	0	2	13

Size: 20-25 in.
Flight speeds: No information

Red-breasted male

Hooded male

Hooded female

HOODED MERGANSER is the smallest and most attractive merganser. It prefers wooded swamps and is rarely seen near salt water. Both male and female show a large crest. Both sexes show white wing patches in flight. The female is dingy gray-brown. These mergansers rise easily in flight and do not run along the water. The nest is always in a tree cavity. It contains 10 to 12 eggs. After the young hatch, they jump to the ground or water. Hooded Mergansers dive well (as do the others) and feed on small fish, tadpoles and crustaceans.

Local names: Swamp Sawbill, Fuzzyhead, Sawbill
Scientific name: *Lophodytes cucullatus*

Weights:	Average		Record	
	lb.	oz.	lb.	oz.
Male	1	8	1	15
Female	1	4	1	8

Size: 16-19 in.
Flight speeds: No information

FOOD FOR WATERFOWL is a key factor in maintaining the population of ducks and geese. Artificial feeding of grain is of occasional help during an emergency. Far more important is the preservation of normal environments where natural plant foods thrive and where migrating or wintering birds can have protection. Restoration of marsh lands, unwisely drained for agriculture, can also help. Steps that control water pollution, silting and flooding also help support waterfowl plant foods. Some waterfowl glean waste grain and sometimes damage grain crops. Diving ducks take more animal food. Major plants used by waterfowl are illustrated on pages 87 and 88. Other foods are listed below.

SOME FOODS OF WATERFOWL

Plant Foods		Animal Foods
Algae (sev. sp.)	Sawgrass	Snails, clams
Baldcypress	Carex	Barnacles
Burreed	Duckweed	Crabs
Naiad	Dock	Crawfish
Corn	Buckwheat	Shrimp
Sorghum	Waterhemp	Grasshoppers
Pigeongrass	Coontail	Crickets
Cutgrass	Watershield	Beetles
Oats	Waterlily	Ants, wasps
Mannagrass	Waterprimrose	Aquatic insect larvae
Barley	Watermilfoil	Minnows
Chufa	Buttonbush	Killifish

seed rootstock

CORDGRASS *(Spartina)* is the main marsh grass of Atlantic and Gulf coasts. Makes salt-hay. Seeds and root stocks eaten.

seed

WIDGEON GRASS, Ditch, or Sea Grass *(Ruppia),* is a common pond-weed of brackish coastal waters. Entire plant is eaten.

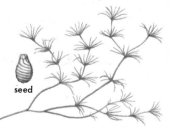

seed

MUSKGRASS *(Chara)* is a lime-coated algae widespread in fresh and brackish waters. Ducks relish the entire plant.

ARROWHEAD or Duck Potato *(Sagittaria)* is abundant in swamps and along river banks. Waterfowl eat tubers and small flat seeds.

seed

seed

SMARTWEED or Knotweed *(Poly-gonum)* is found in uplands as well as in marshes. Seeds are eaten. It is a form of Buckwheat.

PONDWEED *(Potamogeton)* is an important seed-bearing aquatic plant of fresh or slightly saline waters. All parts are eaten.

WATERFOWL FOOD PLANTS 87

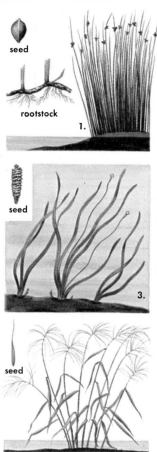

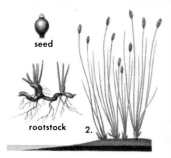

1. **BULRUSH** (*Scirpus*) is a common sedge of ponds, streams and brackish marshes. Varies greatly in appearance. Seeds and stems eaten.

2. **SPIKERUSH** (*Eleocharis*) is a single spiked, nearly leafless, freshwater sedge. Seeds and tubers are eaten.

3. **WILD CELERY** or Eelgrass (*Vallisneria*). Widespread in N.E. ponds and streams. A valuable food; entire plant is eaten.

WILD RICE (*Zizania*) is a tall, plumed grass of marshes and streams. Provides excellent shelter. Seeds are eaten.

WILD MILLET (*Echinochloa*) is a coarse, dense-headed grass which provides shelter as well as large edible seeds.

foot   body form   bill

RAILS

Rails are often called marsh hens. They are chunky, chicken-like birds with short tails and long, strong legs. Of some 129 species, only 10 occur in North America and, of these, seven are considered gamebirds.

North American rails are divided into two groups. The first are seldom-seen birds of dense marshes. They do not swim well and fly poorly with their long legs dangling just over the marsh grasses. Yet this group may migrate over great distances, some wintering in Mexico, Central and South America.

The second includes the coots and gallinules, which are more often seen swimming in open water. Some are mistaken for ducks, but a second look reveals a short, thick, brightly colored bill. Although coots and gallinules are better fliers than other rails, they lack grace and power in the air. They often prefer to spatter along, using wings and feet instead of taking off completely. All rails have loud voices and can be heard grunting and cackling in the marshes. They are difficult to see as they remain hidden in the grass and other vegetation.

short-billed rails   long-billed rails

KING RAIL is one of the largest, with a reddish breast, brown back and long slender bill. A bird of fresh-water swamps, it is seldom seen except during migration. Its flight is weak and fluttering, but during migrations it flies more directly with feet tucked up, usually at night. However, this rail is a resident over much of its range. Its nest, well-concealed in a clump of vegetation, is often arched over with twigs or leaves. In it 8 to 11 pale buff eggs, marked with brown, are laid. These hatch into jet-black chicks which follow their mother until they are fledged. King rails feed mainly on seeds and plants but take insects, frogs and crawfish in summer. Their call is a series of long, rapid "chucks."

Local names: Marsh Hen, Red-breasted Rail, Fresh-water Marsh Hen

Scientific name: *Rallus elegans*

Weights:

	Average		Record	
	lb.	oz.	lb.	oz.
Male	0	11	0	12
Female	No information, probably slightly lighter			

Size: 15-19 in.

Flight speeds: No information

VIRGINIA RAIL is a smaller version of the King Rail with a similar long bill and reddish-brown underparts. These, too, stay deep in fresh-water marshes and are weak fliers, rarely moving more than 5 to 10 yards when flushed. They prefer to escape danger by running rapidly through the marsh grass. During migrations Virginia Rails fly at night and manage to cover long distances. The nest, built in a clump of marsh grass, contains 7 to 12 eggs which require about 15 days to hatch. The day they hatch, the downy, black young can run, swim and dive. Virginia Rails feed mostly on snails, insects, worms and small fish. The call is a rapid series of sharp notes—*tic-it, tic-it*—heard at dawn and dusk.

Local names:	Marsh Hen			
Scientific name:	*Rallus limicola*			
Weights:		Average		Record
		lb. oz.		lb. oz.
Male		0 3.8		0 4.3
Female		0 2.9		0 3.3
Size:	9-10 in.			
Flight speeds:	No information			

CLAPPER RAIL is a bird of salt marshes and was formerly quite common in this habitat. It resembles the King Rail in size and shape, but is gray instead of a rich brown. Like other rails, it is most often seen skulking through the grasses or walking warily along the mud bank of some tidal creek, jerking head and tail with each step. Its narrow, somewhat flattened body aids it in slipping through the vegetation. Good swimmers but weak fliers, they often cross wide tidal channels.

Nests are usually placed on a high spot in the marsh or may be woven into the stalks and leaves some distance above the mud and water. High spring tides endanger the nests and many are destroyed by flooding. Six to 14 eggs are laid which both parents are thought to incubate. In about 14 days the young hatch—small balls of jet-black down.

TWO RARER RAILS

BLACK RAIL is a small (5-6 in.) slate-black bird marked by white spots on its back and faint bars on the abdomen. An uncommon bird of fresh and salt marshes. Sci. name: *Laterallus jamaicensis.*

YELLOW RAIL is only slightly larger than the Black (6-7 in.) but lives in salt- and fresh-water marshes. Has a white wing patch in flight. Sci. name: *Coturnicops noveborancensis.*

Clappers call often in the marsh and a loud noise will often set off a resounding chorus. Their voice is a harsh *cak-cak-cak* repeated in a descending tone. Clappers feed mainly on fiddlers and other small crabs, shrimp, mussels, other small mollusks and small fish. All are eaten avidly. No plant food is taken. Clappers are often hunted from boats poled through the marsh at high tide.

Local names: Marsh Hen, Salt-water Marsh Hen
Scientific name: *Rallus longirostris*
Weights:

	Average		Record	
	lb.	oz.	lb.	oz.
Male	0	12	1	0
Female	0	11	0	12

Size: 14-16 in.
Flight speeds: No information

juvenile

adult

SORA RAIL is the most abundant and widespread N.A. rail, but it is small and often ignored. Note the brownish back, gray underparts, and the black face patch. Soras fly better than other rails and may cover 3,000 miles during migration. Soras nest in fresh-water marshes, laying 10 to 12 eggs in a well-woven nest. Male and female incubate the eggs, which hatch in about 14 days. The black, downy young have a tuft of stiff, yellow chin feathers. In summer, Soras feed on insects, crustaceans and small shellfish. In winter, they take seeds or aquatic plants. Their call is a clear, rapid, descending "whinny," repeated over and over again. Despite their small size, the Sora Rail is an important game species in the Middle Atlantic states.

Local names: Carolina Rail, Rail-bird, Ortolan
Scientific name: *Porzana carolina*

Weights:	Average		Record	
	lb.	oz.	lb.	oz.
Male	0	2	0	3
Female	0	2	0	2.8

Size: 8-10 in.
Flight speeds: No information

Purple

Common

GALLINULES are marginal gamebirds, not often sought by hunters, though they are good eating. The Common Gallinule, the most abundant of the two species, is a duck-like bird with a bright red bill. A patch of white under the tail and a white stripe on the side help identification. It prefers open, fresh-water marshes where it swims and dives well. The brightly colored Purple Gallinule is a southern bird of larger marshes and deeper water. Its long toes support it on lily pads and floating vegetation. Both gallinules nest in the marsh grass, laying 10 to 12 eggs. Gallinules eat marsh plants—mainly seeds but some roots and leaves—and a few small animals.

Local names: Pond Chicken, Blue Peter
Scientific names:
Purple: *Porphyrula martinica*
Common: *Gallinula chloropus*

Weights:	Average		Record	
Common Gallinule				
	lb.	oz.	lb.	oz.
Male	1	0	1	0
Female	0	11	0	12

Purple Gallinule about 3 oz. lighter.
Size: 12-14 in. (both)
Flight speeds: No information

Common Gallinule

Purple Gallinule

COOTS are known to millions as Mud Hens. Hardly a body of fresh water in North America is without coots at least some time during the year. Coots are easily identified by their chunky slate-gray bodies, black heads and white bills. They are the most aquatic members of their family and have developed flaps or lobes on their toes to aid in swimming. This they do well, and dive expertly, too. They are not strong fliers and, when taking off from the water, they patter along for a considerable distance. Once in flight, the white trailing edge of the inner wing is a conspicuous field mark. Coots are hardy and remain in northern marshes until forced out by ice. In spring they return early, arriving soon after the first big thaw.

Coots eat almost anything. They prefer vegetable foods—seeds, leaves and roots of aquatic plants. They also graze on nearby land and may destroy young crops. Animal foods include insects, snails, tadpoles, worms and small fishes. Their voice is loud and varied. Coots make a variety of grunts, squawks, cackling and clucking sounds. Sound tracks of this unusual array of calls from one bird are dubbed into films and tapes to provide "jungle background" for movies and television.

Coots make their nests in dense stands of cattail or bulrushes. The nest is occasionally exposed; sometimes it floats, anchored to nearby vegetation. Both male and female incubate 8 to 12 eggs for about 3 weeks. The downy young swim and dive with their parents.

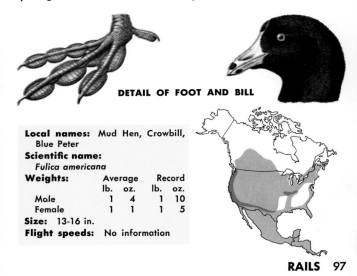

DETAIL OF FOOT AND BILL

Local names: Mud Hen, Crowbill, Blue Peter
Scientific name:
Fulica americana

Weights:	Average		Record	
	lb.	oz.	lb.	oz.
Male	1	4	1	10
Female	1	1	1	5

Size: 13-16 in.
Flight speeds: No information

SHOREBIRDS

Shorebirds are found in wet places throughout the world. There are about 50 North American species including plovers, turnstones, woodcock, snipe and sandpipers. Only two species are considered gamebirds. Most shorebirds are migratory, breeding north to the Arctic and wintering in the far South. During much of the year shorebirds are found in large flocks which include several species. The aerial gyrations of these flocks are an avian wonder.

As a group, shorebirds have long, pointed wings, short tails and long legs. They prefer wet locations, though some have become adapted to drier conditions. All walk or run rapidly; many swim well. Four large, sharply pointed eggs are laid. The protectively colored young run about shortly after hatching. Invertebrates (insects, mollusks and worms) and small fish are principal foods.

COMMON SNIPE, widely distributed in North America, is identified by its boldly striped head and long bill. Snipe prefer wet meadows, marshes and bogs where their brown striped backs make them difficult to see. When flushed, snipe fly low and erratically, giving a harsh *scaipe*. Migrating, they fly high, usually at night. Most are found in the southern states during the winter.

Common Snipe

Dowitcher

spring

winter

The courtship of the snipe includes a flight "song" probably produced by vibrating the outer tail feathers. Four brown, blotched eggs are laid in a grass-lined depression. Both sexes incubate for about 18 to 20 days.

Snipe probe in mud and soft earth with their long bills. Insects make up about half of their diet, with worms, crustaceans and snails also important. Snipe were once abundant. Overshooting has depleted the species, but recent protection has allowed a recovery.

Local names: Jack Snipe, English Snipe
Scientific name: *Capella gallinago*
Weights:

	Average		Record	
	lb.	oz.	lb.	oz.
Male	0	4.2	0	5.5
Female	0	4.2	0	5.5

Size: 10-11 in.
Flight speeds: No information

AMERICAN WOODCOCK is quite common, but rarely seen, throughout much of eastern North America. They rely on their excellent protective coloration and will not flush until almost stepped on. Their long bills, chunky bodies, short necks and tails are distinctive. Unlike most shorebirds, their wings are rounded. Wooded swamps, alder thickets and moist, leafy bottom lands are preferred habitats. The position of the woodcock's eyes is quite unusual—they are set far back and high on the head. This enables the bird to see in a complete circle without moving its head. Migration, governed by the freezing and thawing of the ground, is late in fall and early in spring. When migrating, woodcocks fly low and at night.

The unusual courtship of the woodcock takes place in late evening and early morning when light is very dim. The male finds an open grassy spot and alternates his strutting about with a spectacular spiral flight. During this flight a soft twittering is made, perhaps by the modified wing feathers. No pairing off takes place and one male may mate with several females. The nest, containing four eggs, is a slight hollow in the ground. The female alone incubates for about 21 days. Woodcock fly in two weeks and are fully grown in 25 days. Earthworms are its major food and a bird may consume its own weight daily.

Detail of bill

Detail of wing showing modified primaries

Local names: Timber Doodle,
  Wood Snipe, Bog Sucker
Scientific name: *Philohela minor*

Weights:	Average		Record	
	lb.	oz.	lb.	oz.
Male	0	6.2	0	7.8
Female	0	7.7	0	9.8

Size: 10-12 in.
Flight speeds: 13 mph

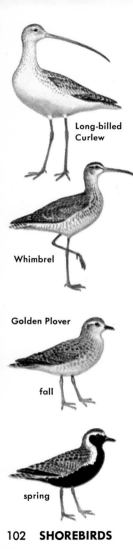

Long-billed Curlew

Whimbrel

Golden Plover

fall

spring

ONCE COMMON SHOREBIRDS

CURLEWS are large, attractive sandpipers, once killed in great numbers. All are tall birds with long down-curved bills. The Eskimo Curlew (*Numenius borealis,* 12-14 in.) may now be extinct. The Long-billed Curlew (*Numenius americanus,* 20-26 in.) is the largest curlew; a bird of the prairie states, it is slowly recovering in numbers. The smaller Whimbrel, or Hudsonian Curlew (*Numenius phaeopus,* 15-18 in.) breeds in the Arctic and migrates along the coasts. It is still the commonest curlew.

AMERICAN GOLDEN PLOVER breeds in the Arctic, then sets a nonstop migratory record over water. Those from the eastern Arctic around Baffin Is. go to southern South America. Those from the western Arctic and Siberia go to central Pacific islands. Breeding plumage is black, flecked with yellow. In winter the birds are brownish and inconspicuous. Once abundant, these birds were almost wiped out by market hunters. Now they are holding their own. Size: 10-11 in.; scientific name: *Pluvialis dominica.*

NO LONGER GAMEBIRDS

GODWITS are large shorebirds with slightly upturned bills. The Marbled Godwit (*Limosa fedoa*, 16-20 in.) is the largest in N.A. These cinnamon birds, with long, pink-based bills, breed on grassy prairies but migrate to the coasts. They feed on lake shores in fall and beaches in winter. The smaller Hudsonian Godwit (*Limosa haemastica*, 14-16 in.) follows the long migration route of the Golden Plover (p. 102). Both species were threatened because of overshooting. Now their numbers are increasing.

UPLAND PLOVER, a slim, graceful bird with a short, thin beak, is not a true plover but belongs to the sandpiper family. These prairie birds spread eastward as forests were cleared, becoming common in fields and pastures. Market hunting in the 1880's and '90's almost wiped them out. This nondescript brownish bird often perches on fence posts, holding wings up for a moment after alighting. Flight swift and buoyant, with down-curved wings. Size: 11-13 in.; scientific name: *Bartramia longicauda*.

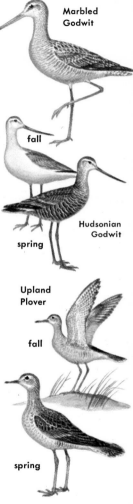

Marbled Godwit

fall

Hudsonian Godwit

spring

Upland Plover

fall

spring

SHOREBIRDS 103

PIGEONS AND DOVES

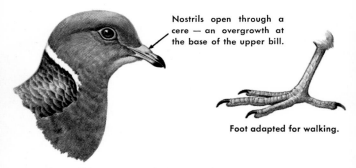

Nostrils open through a cere — an overgrowth at the base of the upper bill.

Foot adapted for walking.

Some 289 species of doves and pigeons have been described by ornithologists, but only nine were regularly found in North America. One of these, the Passenger Pigeon (p. 17) has been extinct since 1914. There is no real difference between pigeons and doves, although the larger species are called pigeons. Most have the general form of the Common Pigeon or Rock Dove—chunky, with a small head and slim bill. Most feed on the ground. Heavy breast muscles and pointed wings provide power for strong, rapid flight.

Pigeons and doves build a fragile nest where one or two white eggs are laid. These are incubated by both sexes for about 14 to 19 days. The young are ready to leave the nest in 12 to 18 days. During the first week the young birds are fed a secretion of the adults' crops called "pigeon milk." The food of pigeons and doves is almost all seeds, fruits and berries. They are quite dependent upon a supply of water. Unlike most other birds, they drink by sucking up water. Only three of the North American species are important gamebirds and of these three the Mourning Dove is outstanding.

Mourning Dove in the East

Local names: Turtle Dove, Long-tailed Dove, Wild Dove

Scientific name: *Zenaidura macroura*

Weights:

	Average		Record	
	lb.	oz.	lb.	oz.
Male	0	4.5	0	6.0
Female	0	4.4	0	5.5

Size: 11-13 in.

Flight speeds: 40 mph

PIGEONS AND DOVES 105

In the Southwest

MOURNING DOVES breed from the southern Canadian provinces to Mexico. Their small heads, slim, streamlined bodies and long, pointed tails are distinctive. Mourning Doves are probably as abundant today as they have ever been. They have benefited by the clearing of forests and the opening of new land.

The food of Mourning Doves is almost entirely weed seeds and waste grain. They prefer small seeds but corn, peanuts and soybeans are taken. Like other doves, they are dependent on water and drink at least once a day.

Mourning Doves are equally at home in the humid East or the arid portions of the West wherever food and water can be found. They are highly migratory, wintering in the southern states and in Mexico. They migrate slowly,

AGE of juvenile birds (wing coverts are light tipped) can be told by the primary feather last moulted. The first one is the innermost.

Primary	Days	Primary	Days
First	40-45	Sixth	91-98
Second	46-56	Seventh	99-115
Third	57-68	Eighth	116-130
Fourth	69-78	Ninth	131-150
Fifth	79-90	Tenth	Over 150

juvenile
under 40 days

In the Southeast

perhaps 15 miles in 24 hours, usually flying in the morning and evening, and feeding during the day.

During the long breeding season a single pair may nest six times. The flimsy nest is usually in a tree or shrub but may be on the ground. Many nest in towns and on farms. Farm shelter belts are favored sites. The two white eggs are incubated by both sexes for about 14 or 15 days. The young squabs are naked when hatched, but grow rapidly and leave the nest in about two weeks. A complete nesting cycle from courtship to fledging takes about one month.

The voice of the Mourning Dove is a soft, five-syllabled coo. Mourning Doves are very important gamebirds. About 20,000,000 are killed annually, more than all waterfowl combined.

juvenile
79-90 days

adult
over 150 days

WHITE-WINGED DOVES with their square tails and white wing patches are unmistakable. They are larger and stockier than Mourning Doves. White-wings are found in the Southwest and throughout Mexico where they are very abundant in some areas. They leave the United States in winter, returning in April. More gregarious than Mourning Doves, they move in flocks even during the breeding season. Nesting takes place in colonies, usually in small dense trees like mesquite or hackberry or even some of the larger cacti. The loose nest of sticks or straw is placed at a junction of limbs from 6 to 20 ft. above the ground. Two buffy-white eggs are laid; one often fails to hatch. The females incubate most of the 15 to 17 days. Probably two broods are raised in each good year and only one in dry seasons. Water is essential to White-wings. Droughts always cause serious population declines.

Males have a soft persistant coo which is often written as "Who cooks for you?" with accent on the last word. During spring and summer the birds are noisy, especially mornings and evenings. Their notes are not loud but carry long distances. Seeds are a major food but fleshy fruits, such as cactus, are often important.

feeding young

Local names: White-wings; Sonora
  Pigeon
Scientific name: *Zenaida asiatica*
Weights:

	Average		Record	
	lb.	oz.	lb.	oz.
Male	0	5.8	0	7.3
Female	0	5.5	0	6.7

Size: 11-12 in.
Flight speeds: No information

BAND-TAILED PIGEON is a bird of western mountains and foothills, preferring an area where there are both oaks and conifers. They like rugged country, with steep slopes and canyons. Their flight is strong and direct. At times they indulge in spectacular dives along the rocky slopes. The compact body, rounded tail and white crescent on the back of the neck are determining field marks. These birds resemble the Rock Dove or Common Pigeon of city streets, but they are birds of tall trees, rarely seen on the ground. They migrate from the northern part of their range in leisurely fashion in late fall. During winter flocks wander widely in search of food. Band-tails nest singly but may also be found in loose colonies. The nest is usually placed on a tree limb but is occasionally on the ground. A single white egg is usually laid but sometimes there are two. Both sexes incubate and brood the young. Incubation takes about 18 days and it is almost a month before the young pigeons leave the nest. During the breeding season males give a loud owl-like hoot or coo, usually of two notes. The summer food consists of berries and fruits; the winter, of acorns and pine seeds. Restricted hunting seasons now protect Band-tails from overshooting.

Band-tailed Pigeon

Rock Dove

Local names: Blue Pigeon, White-
collared Pigeon, Blue Rock
Scientific name: *Columba fasciata*
Weights:

	Average		Record	
	lb.	oz.	lb.	oz.
Male	0	13.1	0	15.5
Female	0	12.8	0	14.0

Size: 15.5 in.
Flight speeds: No information

PIGEONS AND DOVES

GROUND DOVE (6-7 in.) is hardly larger than a sparrow, with a short, sturdy tail. They are often seen on the ground nodding their heads as they walk. Found in pine woods, orchards or along dirt roads in the coastal plains from the Carolinas to Texas, they are quite tame and often come to gardens and bird feeders. When flushed, they fly low and seldom go far before dropping back to the ground. The simple nest is usually in a low bush or on the ground. Two white eggs are incubated for about 12 to 14 days. Small seeds are the most important food. Sci. name: *Columbigallina passerina*.

INCA DOVE, (8 in.) a bird of the arid Southwest, has feathers with dark edgings, making the dove appear scaled. This and the long, white-edged tail are field marks. These small doves can be seen on the ground in parks and gardens in towns. In spring and summer they occur singly or in pairs but in winter they form small flocks. The nest, in a bush or tree, often near houses, is made of fine twigs. Two white eggs are incubated for about two weeks. The Inca Dove has a monotonous double-noted cooing call. Sci. name: *Scardafella inca*.

WHITE-FRONTED DOVE is a large (12 in.) dark-backed, light-bellied bird found from Mexico southward. In the United States it is only seen in the Lower Rio Grande Valley of Texas. This bird of dense brushlands spends most of its time on the ground, but can fly rapidly through thick growth. It never forms flocks. The nest, with 2 eggs, is placed in a low thicket, tangle of vines, or on the ground. White-fronts feed along trails or roads but seldom in the open. Seeds and fruits are their staple diet. Their call is a soft three-noted coo. Sci. name: *Leptohila fulviventris*.

Ground Dove

Inca Dove

White-fronted Dove

WHITE-CROWNED PIGEON, a West Indian species, occurs on the southern tip of Florida and the Florida Keys. The white crown contrasts sharply with its slaty plumage. The flight of these large pigeons (14 in.) is high and direct. White-crowns breed on mangrove islands. The nest is well made for a pigeon, lined with grass, and contains two white eggs. Fruits of many trees are eaten. In the Bahamas and West Indies this bird is an important game species. Sci. name: *Columba leucocephala.*

RED-BILLED PIGEON is a large (13 in.) dark pigeon of Mexico, Central America and south Texas. The tail is broad and rounded, the bill small. The nest is a platform of sticks placed in heavy brush or vines. A single, glossy white egg is usual. Fruits are eaten in summer; seeds and waste grains in winter. Clearing of brush lands may eliminate this pigeon from U.S. Sci. name: *Columba flavirostris.*

GALLINACEOUS GAMEBIRDS

The Gallinaceous or Upland Gamebirds are probably the most important order of birds to man. The common chicken is a prominent member of the group, which includes pheasants, turkeys, quail, and grouse. Of 240 species, some 18 are native to North America and were originally found in almost all habitats. Three more species have been successfully introduced.

In size these chicken-like birds vary from six-ounce quail to 20-pound turkeys. All, however, have plump bodies, large, well-developed breast muscles, and short, thick bills. Their feet are strong and adapted for walking. They scratch for a living and if not pressed too closely, prefer to walk or run rather than fly, though they are capable of strong, rapid flight for short distances. The wings of most species whirr loudly on take-off.

Some gallinaceous birds have adapted to changing conditions and are holding their own or increasing. Others, however, need more specialized habitats and have declined sharply. One, the Heath Hen, a form of Prairie Chicken, has become extinct.

UPLAND GAMEBIRD CLASSIFICATION

North American gallinaceous birds are grouped into three families. The first of these three families contains the grouse. The second family, made up of three subfamilies, encompasses the quail, partridges and pheasants. Finally, the turkeys form a family of their own.

Spruce Grouse

Ocellated Turkey
(Yucatan)

GROUSE (pp. 118-131) are Northern Hemisphere birds with short, down-curved bills and feathered nostrils. Their legs (tarsi) are partly or completely feathered, and the toes of some are also feathered as an aid in walking on soft snow. Most have a bare colored patch over the eye. Males are larger than females and many have large, inflatable air sacs on the neck. Food is mainly leaves, buds, fruits, and some insects.

TURKEYS (pp. 142-144) are large, non-migratory, gregarious New World birds of open woodlands. There are only two species, the Turkey and Ocellated Turkey. Males, much larger than females, have spurs on their bare tarsi. The feet are naked; males have a trace of web between the toes. Bill short; skin of head and neck is bare and brightly colored in male. Flight is strong but of short duration. Food is acorns, fruit, seeds, and insects.

QUAIL (pp. 132-141) are small to medium-sized New World birds which have a single small projection or "tooth" on their bills. Their legs and feet are not feathered and the male has no spur. Both male and female are about the same size. Quail are chicken-like, non-migratory birds. They are monogamous ground-nesters.

Bobwhite

PARTRIDGES (pp. 148-151) are medium-sized Old World birds, plumper than quail. Their bills lack the "tooth" serration. Both feet and legs are free of feathers. All are ground-nesters. Two species have been introduced into North America from Eurasia and are now well established.

Gray Partridge

PHEASANTS (pp. 146-147) are Old World birds, larger than quail and partridges, that reach their maximum development in the highlands of Asia. Legs and feet are bare; males develop large spurs, are larger, and more brightly colored than females. Both have characteristic long, arched tails, better developed in the male.

Ring-necked Pheasant

RUFFED GROUSE are about the size of bantam chickens. Their fan-shaped tails and neck "ruffs" make them easy to identify. Two distinct color phases exist: red, more common in the southern part of the range, and gray in the North and West. Males are larger and more strongly marked than females. In winter both grow horny combs on their toes which act as "snowshoes."

Ruffed Grouse need conifers for winter cover, hardwood and brush for spring and summer, and open spots for dusting and sunning. Abandoned farms and orchards are ideal. In late spring the male stands on a log or stump and makes a loud "drumming" by beating the air rapidly with his wings. Each mates with several females. The nest is on the ground, often near a tree or rock. The female incubates 9 to 12 buffy eggs for about 24 days. Young grouse run about immediately and fly a bit when only 12 days old.

Fruit, leaves and buds make up the diet of adult Ruffed Grouse. The young take many insects. Ruffed Grouse have a varying population cycle. Years of abundance are followed by years of extreme scarcity. Grouse need and often receive protection during the low phase of their population cycle, which seems to occur about every eight to ten years.

TAIL MARKINGS

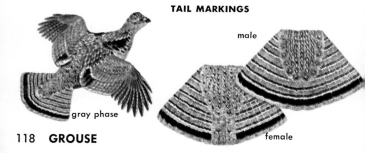

gray phase

male

female

male

female

Local names: Partridge, Pheasant
Scientific name: *Bonasa umbellus*

Weights:

	Average		Record	
	lb.	oz.	lb.	oz.
Male	1	5	1	11
Female	1	2	1	8

Size: 16-19 in.
Flight speeds: 22 mph

GROUSE 119

SAGE GROUSE, the largest North American grouse, is dark gray-brown on the back with a black belly patch and a long, pointed tail. Males are much larger and more distinctly marked than the females. They were formerly abundant in arid sagebrush plains and foothills but farming, grazing, and the systematic destruction of sagebrush have reduced the population greatly. In early spring Sage Grouse gather together in an open strutting ground. Here, at dawn, the males strut and display for prospective mates. They spread their long tails into fans, droop their wings, and inflate and deflate air sacs on the neck and breast, making a strange "plopping" sound. One male may mate with several females.

The nest, a depression under a sagebrush, contains from 7 to 13 olive-buff eggs spotted with brown. These hatch in about 22 days. The young are active very soon after hatching. The female alone incubates the eggs and cares for the young.

Sage Grouse do not have a muscular gizzard like other grouse. Their thin-walled stomachs are adapted to soft foods—the leaves of sagebrush, supplemented in summer by leaves and fruit of other plants as well as grasshoppers and various other insects.

Sage Grouse strutting grounds.

male

female

Local name: Sage Hen
Scientific name: *Centrocercus urophasianus*

Weights:	Average		Record	
	lb.	oz.	lb.	oz.
Male	5	10	8	0
Female	2	10	3	3

Sizes:
Male 28-30 in.
Female 21-22 in.
Flight speeds: 28 mph

GROUSE 121

SHARP-TAILED GROUSE is large with a pointed tail. Its light-brown back is spotted with white and the breast appears streaked. In flight the light tail is conspicuous. Both males and females are alike.

Sharp-tails are found in open brush country or in adjacent prairie. Their numbers fluctuate with the amount of habitat available. Lumbering caused an increase of available open land and hence of birds. This was followed by a decline as forests grew up again. In spring, Sharp-tails gather for courtship dances. The males raise their tails, droop their wings, and run about with short, stamping steps, making low, cooing noises. It is thought that some dances of the Plains Indians may have been patterned after those of the Sharp-tails. In addition, Sharp-tails have a variety of cackling, gobbling calls.

The females nest on the ground, laying from 10 to 13 brown speckled, olive eggs. The yellowish chicks hatch in about 21 days, run about in a few days, and can fly in about two weeks. Insects form an important part of the diet but leaves, flowers and fruit make up the bulk of food consumed. In winter, buds are a major item. Careful management may be necessary to maintain suitable habitat for this species.

Males dancing during courtship.

female

Local name: Sharptail
Scientific name: *Pedioecetes phasianellus*

Weights:	Average		Record	
	lb.	oz.	lb.	oz.
Male	2	1	2	7
Female	1	2	2	3

Size: 17.5 in.
Flight speeds: 33 mph

GROUSE 123

GREATER PRAIRIE CHICKEN is a hen-sized grouse of prairies and grasslands identified by its rounded tail and heavily barred underparts. The Heath Hen (p. 17), an Atlantic coast subspecies, has been extinct since 1932. Since the mid-1800's, when Prairie Chickens were abundant in Midwest prairies, their habitat has been reduced by agriculture and the birds shot until their numbers have declined sharply.

The males gather on "booming grounds" in early spring for courtship and mating. Each male has a territory about 30 feet in diameter where he dances and "booms." The loud calls, produced by orange air sacs, can be heard for a mile. The males stamp their feet, erect their neck feathers, spread out their tails, blow their air sacs, and indulge in battles with their neighbors.

The females lay about 12 eggs in a grass-lined depression. The spotted, olive-buff eggs hatch in about 21 days. The young run around immediately and begin to fly in about two weeks.

Prairie Chickens eat insects, leaves and fruits in summer. Seeds and waste grain are important foods the rest of the year. These grouse have a variety of cackling calls much like those of barnyard chickens.

Booming grounds.

Local names: Pinnated Grouse, Prairie Hens

Scientific name: *Tympanuchus cupido*

Weights:

	Average		Record	
	lb.	oz.	lb.	oz.
Male	2	3	3	0
Female	1	13	2	4

Size: 18 in.

Flight speeds: No information

 LESSER PRAIRIE CHICKEN, a paler, smaller bird of the short grass plains, was formerly found in huge numbers but has diminished greatly. Most now occur in the Panhandle of Texas and adjacent Oklahoma. Their courtship is quite similar to that of the Greater Prairie Chicken. The air sacs on the male are reddish rather than orange, and their "booming" is different in pitch. The nest, well concealed, may contain a dozen creamy, spotted buff eggs. The young resemble those of the Greater Prairie Chicken. Grasshoppers form an important summer food, but seeds and waste grain are important all year.

Local name: Pinnated Grouse
Scientific name: *Tympanuchus pallidicinctus*

Weights:

	Average		Record	
	lb.	oz.	lb.	oz.
Male	1	12	2	0
Female	1	9	1	10

Size: 16 in.
Flight speeds: No information

male

female

BLUE GROUSE of western mountain forests is a large, dark grouse. The male is more strongly marked than the browner female. In summer they prefer aspen groves and willow thickets. In winter they reverse the usual migration pattern and move up the mountains to coniferous forests. The males, in spring, strut like turkeys and "hoot" loudly. Their purplish or yellow air sacs have borders of white feathers. The female lays 7 to 10 buff, spotted eggs in a ground depression. After the young hatch, the female protects them aggressively. In winter these grouse live almost exclusively on conifer needles.

Local names: Gray Grouse, Dusky Grouse, Fool Hen

Scientific name: *Dendragapus obscurus*

Weights:

	Average		Record	
	lb.	oz.	lb.	oz.
Male	2	13	3	8
Female	1	14		

Size: Male: 21 in.; Female: 18 in.

Flight speeds: No information

SPRUCE GROUSE of northern coniferous forests is very tame and easily killed. This tameness gives it the name "Fool Hen." The striking black underparts of the male, barred with white, make it a handsome bird. The female is smaller, browner, and lacks the black belly. Males have a peculiar courtship display. They fly from tree to tree, pausing in the air to make a whirring noise by fluttering their wings.

The females make a grass-lined depression and lay buffy, brown-blotched eggs which hatch in about 17 days. The summer diet of Spruce Grouse includes leaves, fruits, and some insects. In winter, conifer needles are eaten.

Local names: Fool Hen, Spruce Partridge, Canada Grouse				
Scientific name: *Canachites canadensis*				
Weights:	Average		Record	
	lb.	oz.	lb.	oz.
Male	1	4	1	8
Female	0	15	1	1
Size: 15-17 in.				
Flight speeds: No information				

PTARMIGAN are bantam-sized grouse of the Arctic and subarctic tundra. Of our three species, two, the Willow and Rock Ptarmigan, also occur in the Old World. Ptarmigans have superb protective coloration and are quite tame. In summer they are mottled brown, white-winged birds. In winter they turn snowy white and grow hair-like feathers on their feet which aid them in walking over soft snow. They fly swiftly and directly with a burst of speed followed by a long glide. Yet Ptarmigans prefer to walk if not disturbed. In winter large flocks move to lower altitudes, and some migrate for considerable distances over water. These excellent gamebirds are not hunted much because they are so far from most hunters. They do form an important part of the diet of Aleuts, Eskimo and northern Indians who hunt them.

WILLOW PTARMIGANS, largest of three species, are subarctic in distribution. They and the smaller Rock Ptarmigan retain their black tail feathers the year round. In winter the dark eye, bill and tail contrast strongly with the snowy plumage. In spring the male struts and displays for the female, furiously driving away rivals. The nest, on the ground, contains 7 to 10 brown, splotched eggs. Unlike other grouse, the male remains to help raise the chicks. Summer food is leaves, buds and fruits, with some insects. In winter willow buds are eaten.

ROCK PTARMIGAN is slightly smaller than the Willow. It prefers higher elevations and more exposed situations where it is often found far from shelter. The Rock Ptarmigan has strong feet and claws, and scratches through the snow for food. In winter the male shows a black line through the eye. Males battle other males in spring and display for the females. After 6 to 10 eggs are laid in a tundra depression the males depart, but return later.

White-tailed

Rock

Willow

WHITE-TAILED PTARMIGAN is the smallest N.A. species, an alpine bird, living above the timberline and breeding farther south than the two other species. It lacks the black tail of other ptarmigans and in winter is pure white except for dark eye and bill. The nest is in the open, and the incubating female is very reluctant to leave even if the nest is disturbed. From 4 to 15 eggs, usually marked with fine brown dots, are incubated. Feeding habits are the same as for other ptarmigans.

Willow—Red
Rock—Blue
Both—Purple

Local names: (Rock Ptarmigan) Rocker
Scientific names:
Willow: *Lagopus lagopus*
Rock: *Lagopus mutus*
White-tailed: *Lagopus leucurus*
Sizes:
Willow: 15-17 in.
Rock: 13 in.
White-tailed: 12-13 in.
Flight speeds: No information

White-tailed

Rock

Willow

Weights:	Average		Record	
	lb.	oz.	lb.	oz.
Willow:				
Male	—	—	—	—
Female	1	4	—	—
Rock:				
Male	1	3	1	5
Female	1	2	1	4
White-tailed:				
Male	1	2	—	—
Female	0	12	—	—

White-tailed

GROUSE 131

BOBWHITE is probably the most popular gamebird even with those who do not hunt. These small chunky birds and their cheery whistles are familiar to all. When not hunted, Bobwhites become quite tame and often feed near houses. Open pinewoods, brushy fields, abandoned farms, and similar habitats are preferred. Bobwhites usually travel on foot and stay in a limited area. They need food and shelter close together. Hedgerows and shelter belts encourage Bobwhites on farms. Most of the year they stay in coveys of a dozen or more birds. At night the covey roosts in a tight circle, heads out and tails in. This conserves heat in winter and permits fast getaway in danger.

The covey breaks up in spring. Males establish their territories and call the females with their loud *bobwhite*. Pairs build nests on the ground in thick cover, often in high grass. They are well made with an arch of woven grass over the top. The 14 to 16 white eggs hatch in about 23 days. The young birds are thumb-sized but grow rapidly and can fly in two weeks. The males help care for them. Bobwhites are almost omnivorous. Leaves, buds, fruits, seeds, insects and snails all find a place in their diet. Besides the call *bobwhite,* their covey call *quoi-hee* is best known.

FOOD AND SHELTER FOR QUAIL

Bush
Lespediza

Multiflora
Rose

Living fence of Multiflora Rose provides shelter. Bush or Bi-color Lespediza provides food. Such dual plantings are encouraged.

female

male

Local names: Quail, Partridge, Bird

Scientific name: *Colinus virginianus*

Weights:

	Average		Record	
	lb.	oz.	lb.	oz.
Male	0	6	0	9
Female	0	6	0	8.5

Size: 8.5 to 10.5 in.

Flight speeds: Cruising: 28-38 mph
Chased: 44 mph

QUAIL 133

SCALED QUAIL of the arid S.W. lives in sparse grasslands interspersed with cactus, yucca and salt bush. They are most common along dry washes and in valleys. Feathers on the breast and back are edged with black, giving them their scaled appearance. Also called "Cottontops" because of their ragged, bushy, white crests, Scaled Quail need water at least once a day and this limits their range. Dry years may prevent nesting and cause large dips in population. They can fly strongly but prefer walking: they are difficult to flush. Groups of 10 to 40 birds are common; occasionally bands of 100 or more occur. The nesting season coincides with summer

FOODS OF THE DESERT QUAIL

Saltbush or Atriplex

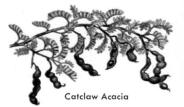

Catclaw Acacia

rains. The nest is a hollow, lined with grass, usually under a bush. Twelve to 14 white eggs, speckled brown, are incubated by the female. The male helps rear the young. Their diet includes shoots, leaves, fruits and insects.

Local names:	Cottontop, Blue Quail		
Scientific name:	*Callipepla squamata*		
Weights:	Average		Record
	lb.	oz.	lb.	oz.
Male	0	7	0	8.2
Female	0	6	0	6.7
Size: 10-12 in.			
Flight speeds:	No information		

Yellow-flowered Prickly Pear

Screwbean Mesquite

CALIFORNIA QUAIL are adaptable, familiar birds of suburban gardens and even city parks. Bold face markings and tilting crests identify the males. These small plump quail prefer open woodlands, chapparal and grassy valleys. With spreading cities and overgrazed ranges, their population has declined but they are still common. This quail runs strongly but will often hide and then flush explosively. These gregarious birds winter in groups of 25 to 60. Bands of 500 to 600 are occasionally found. At night they usually roost off the ground in thickets or trees. Artificial roosts are sometimes supplied for them. The construction of underground water holes has opened habitats unavailable before for these quail.

The nest is a depression in the ground, well hidden and lined with grass. In it are 9 to 14 blotched, cream-white eggs which the female incubates for about 23 days. The male helps rear the young and, if the female is lost, may incubate the eggs. In years of drought, California Quail may not attempt to breed. These vegetarian quail take only about 3% of insects in their diet. The rest is seeds or greens, depending on the season. California Quail have several calls. Perhaps the best known is a loud, three-syllabled *chi-co-go*.

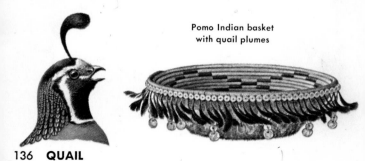

Pomo Indian basket
with quail plumes

male

female

QUAIL 137

GAMBEL'S QUAIL is found only in arid country. It resembles California Quail closely but has a black patch on the belly and more red-brown on the head. It prefers brush, especially thickets of mesquite and hackberry. Originally the fertile river bottoms supported heavy populations but these have dwindled as the land has been cultivated. Gambel's Quail are very strong runners and are flushed with difficulty. In fall and winter they gather in flocks of 20 to 50 or more. In early spring these break up with much fighting among the males as they set up territories. The nest is on the ground, usually under a bush. Ten to 17 eggs, dull white splotched with dark brown, are incubated from 21 to 23 days—mostly by the female. Males do some incubation and help care for the brood. In favorable (wet) years two broods may be raised. In dry years the quail may fail to breed.

The diet of Gambel's Quail is over 90% vegetable. During the brood period insects are taken, but seeds, fruits and greens are favored. Succulent plants help provide water. Like other quail, the Gambel's have many songs and calls, including quiet conversational notes. Most often heard are loud calls similar to the California Quail but higher and more nasal.

GALLINACEOUS GUZZLER
1. Sloping apron collects water.
2. Mouth of underground tank.
3. Roof insulated with soil and rock. 4. Entrance to tank barred to keep out large animals. 5. Fence keeps out livestock.

female

male

Local name: Desert Quail
Scientific name: *Lophortyx gambelii*
Weights:

	Average		Record	
	lb.	oz.	lb.	oz.
Male	0	6	0	7.3
Female	0	5.7	0	6.8

Size: 10-11 in.
Flight speeds: 41 mph
Running speed: 15.5 mph

QUAIL 139

MOUNTAIN QUAIL is the largest and most striking in N. Amer. The chestnut throat and belly, gray breast, barred flanks and long straight crest are unmistakable. They prefer thick brush. Water is very important and they are found not far from it. They do not form large coveys; groups of only 6 to 12 birds are normal. Nests are usually placed under bushes or by rocks or fallen logs. Eight to 12 pale reddish-buff eggs are incubated for about 21 days by both male and female. Males also help care for the young. Mountain Quail eat vegetable food. Seeds, fruits, greens, buds, and even roots are taken. Insects are important early in the brood period. Males have a loud, clear whistle.

Local names: Plumed Quail, Mountain Partridge
Scientific name: *Oreortyx pictus*

Weights:	Average		Record	
	lb.	oz.	lb.	oz.
Male	0	8.2	0	10.2
Female	0	8.2	—	—

Size: 10-11 in.
Flight speeds: No information

male

female

HARLEQUIN QUAIL is found in the pine and oak uplands of the dry S.W. A Mexican species which just reaches the U.S., it prefers scattered brushlands. The striped face, speckled body and bushy crest identify it; females are duller. Harlequin Quail hide when approached and will flush only at the last moment. They place their nests in deep grass and lay 8 to 14 white eggs. Females incubate, but males help rear the chicks. Insects are the main summer diet; roots, seeds and fruits are taken in winter.

Local names: Painted Quail, Fool Quail, Mearn's Quail
Scientific name: *Certonyx monte-zumae*
Weights:

	Average		Record	
	lb.	oz.	lb.	oz.
Male	0	7.3	—	—
Female	0	5.5	—	—

Size: 8 in.
Flight speeds: No information

Mountain Quail

Harlequin Quail

TURKEYS are the kings of North American upland gamebirds. Widely used by Indians, they were domesticated in Mexico long before Columbus arrived. Taken to Spain, they spread through the Near East, perhaps acquiring the misnomer of "turkey" on the way. Native turkey populations declined steadily with settlement and agriculture. The birds now occupy only a fraction of their original range.

Wild birds are slimmer, darker, and more streamlined than domestic ones. Both sexes have a "beard"—a hairlike tuft of breast feathers. This is more developed in the male, which also has more head color and more iridescence in its feathers. Females are smaller and lighter. Turkeys prefer open woods with clearings or western park land. They need brushy cover, water and a supply of acorns, beechnuts, wild grapes, dogwood, and other fruits. They take grain, seeds and, in summer, large insects.

During most of the year gobblers flock together away from the hens and young. Flocks roost in trees, feeding in early morning and late evening. In early spring each gobbler establishes his territory where he struts and gobbles. The hens soon come and, after the usual fighting with rivals, each gobbler sets up a harem of several hens.

Rio Grande subspecies

Eastern subspecies

Local name: None
Scientific name: *Meleagris gallopavo*
Weights:

	Average		Record	
	lb.	oz.	lb.	oz.
Male	16	5	23	13
Female	9	5	12	5

Size: Male: 48 in.
Female: 36 in.
Flight speed: 55 mph

TURKEYS 143

Merriam subspecies

Each hen nests in a slight depression near a clearing, laying from 8 to 15 buff, finely spotted eggs. The hen alone incubates for 28 days, then broods the active young which are able to fly and roost in trees in about 4 weeks.

Turkeys prefer walking and running to flight, but, when pressed or startled, fly strongly and directly, usually rising at steep angles and gliding off for considerable distances. Turkeys are wary, nervous birds that keep constantly on the move. Their restoration as gamebirds depends on man's maintaining of large stretches of open woodlands with oak, beech, nut pines, and wild fruits, which the birds need. Four subspecies occur in the U.S.

Florida subspecies   domestic turkey

Importation of pheasants in 1790.

EXOTIC GAMEBIRDS were introduced into North America even before Benjamin Franklin's son-in-law tried to establish partridges and pheasants in New Jersey in 1790. Hundreds of other attempts were made in hopes that exotic birds would take the place of fast-disappearing native species. Most attempts were failures (pp. 152-153) and to date only three species have been successfully established. Generally speaking, the chances of success are limited when native species are doing well in the same environment and can compete directly with the introduced species. Success may also be limited unless the new environment is very much like the one in which the exotic species has prospered. Finally, a large enough introduction must be made to give the new birds a chance to build up populations in the face of normal mortality.

Two of our three successful exotic species can get along with the intensive agriculture that has doomed most upland gamebirds. But even the Ring-necked Pheasant and the Gray Partridge need help. This is provided when hedgerows and windbreaks are reinforced with shelter and food plants, and when farm practices leave winter fields with waste grain for the birds. The Chukar Partridge, whose success has been more limited, is able to live on rough, barren mountain slopes of the Southwest where there are few native gamebirds. These successful species provide game in areas where it would otherwise be lacking.

female

male

RING-NECKED PHEASANTS were first successfully introduced in 1881 though attempts had been made nearly a century before. The years that followed saw many transplants of different strains of pheasants, some with ringed necks, some without. Present American stock is a mixture of several strains. Pheasants are now firmly established, doing best in the cornbelt and on irrigated western farmlands. Because of the heat or other less understood reasons, they do not survive in the dry Southwest, or in the moister Southeast. The gaudy plumage and long arched tail of the cock pheasant are unmistakable. Hens are smaller and show a subdued pattern of brown, buff and black. They, too, have long tails. Pheasants need varied habitats—mixtures of cropland, grassland and brush are best. In winter they form small loose flocks in which the sexes are more or less segregated. Large numbers may congregate in areas where food and shelter are good. Pheasants usually prefer

to run when disturbed, though they can fly strongly for short distances. In spring the cocks establish territories and defend them fiercely. Each is joined by several hens which nest in well-concealed hollows, incubating 6 to 16 dull greenish eggs for 22 to 23 days. The chicks grow rapidly and can fly in two or three weeks. Pheasants feed mainly on waste grain, weed seeds, wild fruits and insects. The "crow" of the cock is like an old-fashioned automobile horn—a raucous *ah-oogah*.

Local names: Ring-neck, English Pheasant, Chinese Pheasant

Scientific name: *Phasianus colchicus*

Weights:

	Average		Record	
	lb.	oz.	lb.	oz.
Male	2	11	4	0
Female	2	2	3	3

Size: Male: 30-36 in.
Female: 21-25 in.

Flight speeds: Cruising: 27-38 mph
Chased: 60 mph

GRAY PARTRIDGES were not successfully introduced until the late 1800's despite several earlier attempts. This common European gamebird does well in habitats that will not support native species. It prefers a cool, somewhat dry climate and seems to thrive on open, cultivated lands, as in the north central states and adjacent Canada. Even in severe winter weather Gray Partridges can be found in the open searching for waste grain. The gray breast, chestnut belly patch and short chestnut tail are good field marks. Gray Partridges usually fly low and fast, alternating bursts of wing beats with coasting on stiffly arched wings. In winter they move in coveys of 20 to 30 birds. With spring the birds pair off, the males fighting continually. Later each pair goes off to nest, making a shallow depression lined with grass. The female lays 9 to 20 olive eggs which she incubates alone for about 24 days, covering the eggs with grass and leaves when she leaves the nest. The male stays nearby and later helps care for the young. The Gray Partridge feeds primarily on grain gleaned from harvested fields. It takes wheat, barley, corn and oats, seeds of weeds and grasses, and some wild fruits. A few insects are eaten in summer. The call of this partridge is a harsh *kee-ah*.

FOOD OF GRAY PARTRIDGE

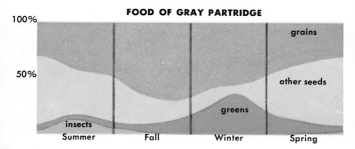

100%

50%

grains

other seeds

greens

insects

Summer   Fall   Winter   Spring

Local names: Hungarian Partridge, Hun, Hunkie, European Partridge

Scientific name: *Perdix perdix*

Weights:

	Average		Record	
	lb.	oz.	lb.	oz.
Male	0	14	1	0
Female	0	13	0	15

Size: 12-13 in.

Flight speeds: Cruising: 27 mph
Chased: 53 mph

PARTRIDGES 149

CHUKAR PARTRIDGE, native of dry southeastern Europe and parts of Asia, was first brought to North America in 1893. Early attempts at introduction were failures and even after repeated efforts the bird is not too well established. It needs semi-arid, open, rocky country and so has done best in parts of the West where adequate water is available. Chukars are handsome birds, between quail and grouse in size, easily recognized by their striking face pattern and barred flanks. They fly strongly but, unless approached from above, prefer to escape by running uphill. During summer, when water is especially important, they are seldom found far from it. The rest of the year they are more widespread. Flocks of 10 to 40 birds are the rule. Chukars prefer to roost on the ground, in the open or among rocks. In spring the birds pair off and, as soon as the eggs are laid in a hollow near a rock or bush, the males go off to form their own groups. The females incubate the creamy, brown speckled eggs for 21 to 22 days. Later the males return and help care for the young. Chukars feed mainly on weed seeds, wild fruits, leaves, and bulbs. The bulbs are dug out with their bills. Seasonally, insects, especially grasshoppers, are important. The common call gives the birds their name.

Chukar Partridge   Rock Partridge   Red-legged Partridge

Local name: Rock Partridge
Scientific name: *Alectoris graeca*
Weights:

	Average		Record	
	lb.	oz.	lb.	oz.
Male	1	4	1	8
Female	1	2	1	4

Size: 13 in.
Flight speeds: No information
Running speed: 18 mph

GAMEBIRD INTRODUCTIONS

Spotted Dove
Asia

Rufous-winged Tinamou
South America

Baikal Teal
Asia

Capercaillie
Eurasia

Black Cock
Europe

Within a century after the discovery of America attempts at introducing new wildlife were made. These haphazard introductions continued for 300 years until the U.S. Fish and Wildlife Service took control of the situation in 1900. Lack of knowledge made most of these attempts failures. At best the efforts were costly and uncertain. Some introduced forms damaged crops and competed with valued native species. Only a few have found a place for themselves here. These have been included on previous pages.

For fifty million years birds have drifted into new environments. Some

SOME ATTEMPTED

Capercaillie
Chachalaca
Cock, Black
Crake, Corn
Curassow
Dove, Australian Crested
Dove, Bleeding Heart
Dove, Spotted
Dove, Ring-necked
Dove, Rock
Francolin, Common
Goose, Egyptian
Grouse, Hazel
Grouse, Sand
Guinea Fowl
Partridge, Bamboo
Partridge, Red-legged

have survived and developed in them. The slow sifting process of evolution has gradually placed most birds in their best environments. New and sudden introductions rarely consider all the factors involved if a bird is to prosper in an unoccupied or newly created habitat. Long study of the bird in its original habitat and detailed study of the new are needed. This includes a full knowledge of food, shelter and nesting habits, disease resistance, competitive species and possible enemies.

Below are listed some of the attempted gamebird introductions in the United States that have not been successful. Many other species have also been tried.

INTRODUCTIONS

Pheasant, Black-backed Kaleege
Pheasant, Copper
Pheasant, Golden
Pheasant, Lady Amherst
Pheasant, Mongolian
Pheasant, Reeves
Pheasant, Silver
Pheasant, Trapogan
Quail, Button
Quail, Coturnix
Quail, Elegant
Swan, Mute
Teal, Baikal
Teal, Common
Tinamou (Tinamus robustus)
Tinamou, Rufous-winged
Turkey, Oscellated

Reeves Pheasant
Asia

Coturnix Quail
Eurasia

Lady Amherst Pheasant
Asia

Mute Swan
Europe

153

Diking a waterfowl marsh.

HABITAT IMPROVEMENT

In recent years wildlife management has pointed the way to increase the populations of gamebirds. Early efforts were triggered by the drastic decline of many species in the late 1800's. These efforts included artificial propagation of stock and the introduction of substitute exotic species. Research now shows that the most suitable way to increase the gamebird population is through habitat improvement. When natural environments are drastically changed or reduced, a drop in gamebirds inevitably follows. When the environment is again made favorable,

Brush pile feeding station.

Forest clearing increases food plants.

populations build up. This principle can be applied to many types of habitat. Wetlands are essential to all waterfowl. In past years too many marshes and sloughs were drained. With the establishment of a continent-wide refuge system and the restoration of wetlands, duck populations have partially recovered. Farming practices detrimental to upland gamebirds can be mitigated by leaving brush in fence rows, planting living fences, establishing food patches, and excluding grazing cattle from woodlands. Enclosed corners of pastures which allow brush and weeds to grow provide food and shelter for quail. Where winters are severe, evergreen plantings provide shelter. The building of brush piles, roosts, or watering holes may also be effective. Forest clearings encourage a variety of plants which provide diversified shelter and more plentiful food. Even fire can be useful. Properly controlled it maintains certain habitats like southern pine forests and midwestern prairies.

Habitat improvement is carried on mainly by state fish and game or conservation departments. Trained game managers develop projects on public land and advise and assist persons or groups who want to try such practices on private land.

BOOKS FOR MORE INFORMATION
ABOUT GAMEBIRDS

Field Guides and Surveys

Kortright, F. H., Ducks, Geese & Swans of N. Amer., Stackpole, 1953
Leopold, A. S., Wildlife of Mexico, U. of Cal. Press, Berkeley, 1959
Peterson, R. T., Field Guide to the Birds, Houghton, 1947
Peterson, R. T., Field Guide to Western Birds, Houghton, 1961
Pough, R. H., Audubon Water Bird Guide, Doubleday, 1951
Pough, R. H., Audubon Western Bird Guide, Doubleday, 1957
Rand, A. L., American Water & Game Birds, Dutton, 1956

Life Histories and Reports

Bent, A. C., Life Histories of N. Amer. Wild Fowl (Parts 1 & 2), U.S.
Nat. Mus. Bulls. 126 & 130, Washington, D. C., 1925, 1927
Life Histories of N. Amer. Shore Birds (Part 1), U.S. Nat. Mus. Bull.
142, Washington, D.C., 1927
Life Histories of N. Amer. Gallinaceous Birds, U.S. Nat. Mus. Bull.
162, Washington, D.C., 1932
Bump, G., R. Darrow, F. Edminster & W. Cressy, The Ruffed Grouse,
N. Y. State Conserv. Dept., Albany, N. Y., 1947
Hochbaum, H. A., Canvasback on a Prairie Marsh, Wildlife Mgmt.
Inst., Washington, D.C., 1959
Sowles, L. K., Prairie Ducks, Wildlife Mgmt. Inst., Wash., D.C., 1955
Stoddard, H. L., The Bobwhite Quail, Scribners, New York, 1943

Conservation and Management

Allen, D., Pheasants in N. Amer., Wildlife Mgmt. Inst., Wash., D.C.,
1956
Edminster, F. C., American Game Birds of Field & Forest, Scribners,
New York, 1954
Martin, A. C., H. S. Zim & A. L. Nelson, American Wildlife & Plants,
McGraw-Hill, New York, 1951
McAtee, W. L., Ring-Necked Pheasant and Its Management in N.
Amer., Wildlife Mgmt. Inst., Washington, D.C., 1945
Mosby, H. S. & C. O. Handley, The Wild Turkey in Virginia, Comm.
Game & Inland Fisheries, Richmond, 1943
Schwartz, C. W., Ecology of the Prairie Chicken in Missouri, U. of
Missouri Studies, 20, No. 1, Columbia, Missouri, 1945
Wright, B. S., High Tide and an East Wind (Black Duck), Wildlife Mgmt.
Inst., Washington, D. C., 1954

NATIONAL WILDLIFE REFUGES

There are about 290 National Wildlife Refuges in the United States. These total 28½ million acres. Some of the larger or better known ones, well worth visiting, are listed below. A map of some of these refuges is on p. 12. Visitors are welcome. A complete list with addresses can be obtained from the U.S. Fish and Wildlife Service, Washington 25, D.C.

ALABAMA: Wheeler. **ALASKA:** Aleutian Islands, Kenai National Moose, Kodiak. **ARIZONA:** Havasu Lake, Imperial (also California), Kofa Game Range. **CALIFORNIA:** Merced, Sacramento, Salton Sea, Tule-Klamath Lake. **COLORADO:** Monte Vista. **DELAWARE:** Bombay Hook. **FLORIDA:** Chassahowitzka, Great White Heron, Key Deer, Key West, Loxahatchee, Sanibel, St. Marks. **GEORGIA:** Blackbeard Island, Okefenokee, Piedmont, Savannah (also South Carolina). **ILLINOIS:** Cautauqua, Crab Orchard, Mark Twain (also Iowa and Missouri). **IOWA:** Union Slough. **KANSAS:** Kirwin, Quivera. **KENTUCKY:** Kentucky Woodlands. **LOUISIANA:** Delta, Lacassine, Sabine. **MAINE:** Moosehorn. **MARYLAND:** Blackwater. **MASSACHUSETTS:** Monomoy, Parker River. **MICHIGAN:** Seney, Shiawassee. **MINNESOTA:** Agnassiz, Rice Lake, Tamarac, Upper Mississippi River (also Illinois, Iowa, Wisconsin).

MISSISSIPPI: Gulf Islands, Noxubee, Yazoo. **MISSOURI:** Mingo, Squaw Creek, Swan Lake. **MONTANA:** Benton Lake, Bowdoin, Ft. Peck Game Range, Medicine Lake, National Bison Range, Red Rock Lakes. **NEBRASKA:** Crescent Lake, DeSoto (also Iowa), Ft. Niobrara, Valentine. **NEVADA:** Desert, Ruby Lake, Stillwater. **NEW JERSEY:** Brigantine, Troy Meadows. **NEW MEXICO:** Bitter Lake, Bosque del Apache. **NEW YORK:** Elizabeth Morton, Montezuma, Oak Orchard. **NORTH CAROLINA:** Mattamuskeet, Pea Island. **NORTH DAKOTA:** Arrowwood, Des Lacs, Lake Ilo, Long Lake, Lostwood, Lower Souris, Slade, Snake Creek, Sullys Hill, Tewaukon, Upper Souris. **OKLAHOMA:** Salt Plains, Tishomingo. **OREGON:** Malheur, Sheldon-Hart Mt. (also Nevada). **PENNSYLVANIA:** Erie. **SOUTH CAROLINA:** Cape Romain, Carolina Sandhills, Santee. **SOUTH DAKOTA:** Lacreek, Lake Andes, Sand Lake, Waubay. **TENNESSEE.** Reelfoot, Tennessee. **TEXAS:** Aransas, Buffalo Lakes, Hagerman, Laguna Atascosa, Muleshoe, Sana Ana. **UTAH:** Bear River, Fish Springs. **VERMONT:** Missisquoi. **VIRGINIA:** Back Bay, Chincoteague, Presquile. **WASHINGTON:** Columbia, Little Pend Oreille, McNary, Turnbull, Willapa. **WISCONSIN:** Horicon, Necedah. **WYOMING.** National Elk, Hutton Lake.

Asterisks (*) denote pages on which the subjects are illustrated.

The pages indicated in **boldface type** are those containing the major text treatment and most extensive information.